ADVAN

G000112056

"Matt Stephen's book *The Engagement Revolution* is a pragmatic, provocative and lucid book with plenty of real life case examples of bringing employee engagement into the 21st century. It not only informs, but engages, and will teach you how to do the same."

Steven D'Souza
Associate Fellow, University of Oxford,
co-author of *Not Knowing*

"*The Engagement Revolution* sets out a bold new process of encouraging engagement for a new world of work! Matt Stephens gets to the heart of engagement – measuring what really matters in real time!"

Marshall Goldsmith
New York Times bestselling author of *Triggers, MOJO*
and *What Got You Here Won't Get You There*

"Heart beating, muscles pumping, mind racing … is your business fit to win in today's world? Matt Stephens gives you the fresh inspiration and practical tools to engage your people more deeply, to find your energy and rhythm, to deliver positive change and high performance."

Prof Peter Fisk
Professor of Strategy, Innovation and Marketing, IE Business School, and author of *Gamechangers*

"Analytics today allows us to do so many things because of its high intelligence quotient (IQ), but it is low in its emotional quotient (EQ). Inpulse has found a way of bridging that gap by adding the missing layer of emotional intelligence to our understanding of engagement. With Inpulse you can clearly see that how people feel impacts their engagement and the case studies in this book provide a rich source of evidence and applicable data, to prove this very profound principle."

Mike Bugembe
Chief Analytics Officer, JustGiving, and author of *Finding Value in Data*

"*The Engagement Revolution* provides insight and advice on improving employee performance, something that is vital for the technological age."

Russ Shaw
Founder, Tech London Advocates
and Global Tech Advocates

"Measuring and understanding the impact of engagement in an organization is essential to its success and we need to develop our insight frameworks to build a true picture of how our people are feeling. *The Engagement Revolution* offers a vital new model and approach to help organizations understand the emotions of their people, as ultimately, understanding emotions enables organizations to build honest and open conversations – an essential foundation for organizational performance."

Jennifer Sproul
Chief Executive, Institute of Internal Communication

Published by
LID Publishing Limited
The Record Hall, Studio 204,
16-16a Baldwins Gardens,
London EC1N 7RJ, UK

info@lidpublishing.com
www.lidpublishing.com

A member of:

BPR
Business Publishers Roundtable

www.businesspublishersroundtable.com

First edition published in 2017 under the title
Revolution in a Heartbeat

Printed in Great Britain by TJ International
ISBN: 978-1-912555-37-6

Cover and page design: Caroline Li & Matthew Renaudin

MATT STEPHENS

THE ENGAGEMENT REVOLUTION

USING EMOTIONAL INSIGHTS TO DRIVE BETTER BUSINESS PERFORMANCE

MADRID | MEXICO CITY | LONDON
NEW YORK | BUENOS AIRES
BOGOTA | SHANGHAI | NEW DELHI

CONTENTS

Foreword and Acknowledgments

Since I wrote *The Engagement Revolution*, more and more corporate companies have joined in the revolution. Against all expectations, measuring emotion and having a transparent, real-time survey is beginning to become the norm!

This book is not meant to simply be a way of cheerleading for the Inpulse platform, which measures employee engagement in real time. It is meant to be a way of stirring up the 'People vs. Emotional Analytics' debate, challenging mindsets about engagement and, most of all, showing what is possible when brave people take a risk and try a new approach. I'm thrilled to see how many people not yet associated with Inpulse have endorsed the book and recognize that the path we're travelling is the right one. It's also heartening to know you're not alone, and for that I'm eternally grateful to the companies that became early adopters of Inpulse and have taken on the new approach of listening and leading that Inpulse advocates.

Inpulse's early clients were the adopters of new technology, and at the vanguard of the future approach to emotional analytics. It takes bold people to agree to run surveys that have total transparency. Those who agreed to be case studies for the book can't be thanked enough. Without their evidence and stories, we wouldn't have been able to prove what we already thought to be true: emotions matter, transparency is key and real time is critical.

My own business has gone through a massive acceleration since I wrote this book. We have new team members and a new office. But most of all, it's exciting to think how much

Inpulse is changing. It undergoes its own revolution regularly, as the software and approach are adjusted and adapted to what we learn from our clients. This means we are living our own brand by challenging and adapting as the future becomes reality.

The future is about measuring emotion, being transparent with the results, focusing on the employee experience, and expecting more of our leaders and the conversations we have with them. The faster companies get on-board with these changes to the people landscape of our organizations, the faster they will grow and evolve. We're on the right track – so why not come join this revolution and see where it leads us?

First and foremost, huge thanks must go to John Simmons, a good friend, madcap Arsenal fan and the best writer I know. John and I collaborated on writing this book and without his guidance, knowledge, experience and friendship (and the odd bit of nagging), it wouldn't have happened. Thank you, John, for your thoughts, words and edits, but most of all for your continuing friendship and collaboration. To the Inpulse team, I think you're fantastic and I couldn't have done this without you; I love what we're becoming and where we're going – let the adventure continue! In particular, to Dominic Walters, Director of Coaching, our conversations about leadership were invaluable, as is your friendship and support. To Dan Singerman for all your help, support and technical genius – it's greatly appreciated. To Marcelo Borges, Peter Collyer, Natasha Liedl-McDowall,

Edith Wilkinson, Lesley Swarbrick and Paul Phillips, thank you for contributing to the book, but most of all for believing in Inpulse – I appreciate you 'jumping in' and talking candidly about your experiences. To LID Publishing, for all the amazing work you've done in making sure the book is as good as it could be and taking a risk on a new author.

To Steve Martin, Mike Bugembe, Andrew Cherrie and Gavin Poole, for your friendship and encouragement, for providing a sounding board for thoughts about Inpulse and business more generally, and for spurring me on to greater things.

Finally, to Amanda, my business partner, confidant and best friend. Thank you for all you carry and for letting me be me and come up with these crazy ideas and then develop them! Without your steady hand on the finances, thoughtful mind and encouragement to keep believing, we wouldn't be here with dozens and dozens of clients using something that only existed as an idea in my mind a couple of years ago.

CHAPTER 1

The Why Factor

After 40 years on planet Earth, my view is that human beings are driven by emotion, not reason. With 20 years in business, leading people, managing complex projects and working with leaders at all levels, I can think of hundreds of situations where facts, reason and logic have failed to sway, influence or 'move' someone to a different action or mindset. My conclusion, in business as in life, is that your message, your communication, your desire to get the best from someone – let's say 'engage' someone to get the best from them – has to focus on emotions, while maintaining a balance between logic and feelings. Emotions create movement and action, they generate pride towards a company and hope and excitement for the future. Yes, we are persuaded by logic, but we're moved by emotion. So we need to understand and maybe even measure emotion. And just as importantly, why people feel the way they do. In his book *Emotional Intelligence*, Daniel Goleman says that understanding emotions is more important in leading a successful life than having high intelligence. His assertion is that emotional intelligence largely determines our success in relationships, work and human relations skills.

Let's Take Work

It occupies most of our life.

Of course, there are the competing calls of family, friends and interests outside our working hours. But if we are to have a life, and a fulfilling life, those hours in the week when we work need to give us a reward and a reason for the large chunk of our time, energy and thoughts that they consume.

That time matters. As employees or employers, we should be concerned with making the working experience as emotionally rich as possible.

Earning money remains the most important reason why we go to work. But increasingly, we recognize that good companies offer more than just pay cheques. We can choose between employers – and in a fluid labour market we choose more frequently than we ever used to – so our experience matters.

There are emotional, not just financial, reasons for making that choice. There is a two-way contract, to do the best you can for each other. *So be fair to me. Listen to me.* Persuade me. Involve me. It's an emotional contract more than a legal one, built on persuasion, not compulsion.

So what must a good company do to make sure it attracts, keeps and motivates the people who are essential to its performance and future growth? How can it make sure that its people are not just *at* work, but fully committed, intellectually and emotionally, to their work? How can your company fully engage people's minds and emotions?

The first answer is to determine what they are really thinking and feeling about their experience of being part of the company, to take the first brave step of seeking the truth.

"How are you feeling about working here? Why do you feel this way?" To ask such questions is not 'fluffy', as might once have been the dismissive description. These are existential questions for a company in the 21st century. Step by step, companies have been moving from a 20th-century model based on command and control to a model fit for this century that recognizes the need to be emotionally connected to a company's purpose.

Over the last 20 years, the total value of an enterprise has shifted from the so-called tangible (i.e. easily measurable) assets of a business (plant, machinery, etc.) to the intangible, particularly human and knowledge capital. On average, around 70% of value is in this intangible domain, as opposed to 20% to 30% 20 years ago.
(Source: Institute for Employment Studies.)

Therefore, we are becoming more human in our working environment. This suggests we are more openly emotional: "Do I want to do what you've asked me to? How do I feel about what the leader has just said?" The huge difference is in acknowledging that an individual's emotional and intellectual energy can and should impact the business strategy.

Alongside this, we now have a significantly more diverse workforce than ever before. Imagine the scale of differing hopes and dreams and the variety of emotional styles involved. So, understanding how people feel and why, or to put it another way, *how* engaged and motivated employees feel, becomes critical to the business.

An example of this shift in approach is the 'annual employee engagement survey'. The very idea – if we could drop back 40 years in time – might once have seemed progressive, coming from the place of "we want to find out if our employees feel really engaged in what we do."

Annual surveys were carried out to reveal the views of their employees. It was a breakthrough at the time, but we have since moved on; culture and technology have changed. Yet companies still have the same form of annual survey embedded into their business cycle as 'things we must always do'.

The need to test the temperature regularly is well established. Employers want to find out how much employees identify and emotionally connect their own aims, purpose and desires with those of the company. The annual employee engagement survey has become the accepted, now traditional, means to do that. I know, because I have initiated many such surveys in companies myself.

After all, we might say, it's good to show willingness, and we are doing no harm in trying to do some good. Yet always, when faced with a situation of ingrained acceptance,

I personally feel the need to challenge and probe. The only way to do this is by asking questions. Actually, one question is enough to start the process. The question is "why?"

Why?

'Why' is always the most powerful question, aiming straight to the heart of a problem. As such, it often leads to more questions: What? When? How? Where? These are all useful questions, which create the foundation of a plan. But these questions have a tendency towards answers that are primarily rational and factual.

A company meeting.
At 9.30, first Monday of May.
Organized by HR.
In the atrium.

Useful, but those facts – and others that companies feel comfortable about adding – will not tell you much about the question you really need to answer. Not just 'how' are they feeling, but 'why'.

'Why' is the match that sparks an emotional reaction, which leads to a moment of enlightenment and understanding and shows that something needs to be done.

'Why' is the precursor to 'because'.

Contained in the word '*because*' is the word '*cause*', and this goes to the heart of discovering what a good company really wishes to know. What is the cause of your engagement or lack of engagement in what this company is aiming to do? Are you with us or not? '*Why*'?

The answers are a rich source of data, so much richer than if the questioning stopped before '*why*'. Annual employee surveys are one way to attempt to get that information, but the information comes filtered by time and difficulties in responding honestly and spontaneously. The questioning is extensive, but not insightful. The truth is lost in data overload and in a rush to seek a score, a percentage, without really pushing for the simple, elegant clarity of '*why*'. It becomes easier for the respondents to give less emotional, less candid answers.

Data is useless without action.

Companies have become skilled accumulators of data, taking it and turning it into meaningless numbers. "We are 0.34653 better than last year; let's celebrate!" Sounds like madness, but an amazing amount of this goes on in boardrooms around the world.

But what will they actually do with it? What does 0.34653 actually mean? How are our people feeling? And why? What has been their experience?

Part of the problem is connected to time. Companies gather information, analyse it, put it into tables and percentages for year-on-year comparison, then nod knowingly across a boardroom table when the results are presented several months after the questions were originally asked.

In the meantime, the context has changed. The same questions asked at this later point would elicit different responses. Different questions might even be needed. Cynicism might have set in among people who were asked questions, yet their answers seem to have received no response. And yet the data will be used to make decisions to do with employees long after it becomes invalid and useless ... which at the longest is a few months later.

The perception is:
Silence = no comment = we are ignoring you.

To be fair, many leaders and managers know this. It's a bit like sending a message across the ocean in a boat when we can send it instantly instead. It's a truism that "we live in a fast-moving world". There's no arguing with that, but it doesn't mean we have to cling to slowness. A slow response is nearly always dangerous because it will be interpreted by many as a reluctant response, possibly even a dishonest one. There must be a better way.

We need data that simply and easily reveals clear insights into what employees think, feel and experience.

Is this possible? Yes it is!

Companies need to learn from changes in the world around them. Learn from politics, from social media and from what the 21st century is telling us.

Yes, we do live in fast-moving times. Such times demand greater speed. They also, crucially, demand greater transparency. Employees no longer automatically believe what they are told by their employers. They believe in their own judgments based on their own emotions, what they see and hear, and the actions their leaders take, not what they say. The age of deference is over.

Find a better way of listening to your employees and understanding what they have to say. To make better decisions, have better conversations based on what people are really feeling and thinking.

From this way of thinking, a number of vital principles emerged and a thought process was developed that responds to real experiences encountered in workplaces, with some of the biggest companies around. The best were eager to find a better way, so I started to drill down into the problem further, attempting to find a positive solution.

From that thinking, a number of words stood out like landing lights seen from a distance. Could these words guide us towards a better way of communicating? Could we form principles around them?

Words such as …

Heart.

Emotion.

Transparency.

Experience.

Instant.

Conversation.

Why these words? What principles might lie behind them? Let's explore a little further.

Heart Is the Universal Human Metaphor

"It's a matter of the heart." "I committed to it, heart and soul." "He really didn't have his heart in it." "She'll do what her heart tells her to do."

None of these common phrases depict the heart in its literal state, as a muscle that pumps blood through the body. But in every culture, in every language, human beings refer to the heart as the essential and real part of each of us, a way of feeling and expressing our most genuine, revealing emotional states.

We recognize the brilliance of this graphic device by Milton Glaser, which has since been copied by countries and cities worldwide, displayed on billions of T-shirts. But, of course, we respond to it because we recognized it from a point much further back. It's a symbol as old as time. It would be no surprise to discover that early humans painted it on the walls of caves as, in more modern historical times, people have scratched it into the bark of trees.

"Run, run, Orlando: carve on every tree."

William Shakespeare, *As You Like It*

We all have hearts and we all have a pulse. The pulse is the way we measure the activity of our actual heart and its responses to different experiences and moments as they happen. You need a rhythm, a regularity, a pulse check to know how people are feeling by gathering responses that are spontaneous and naturally emotional.

Emotion Needs to Be Embraced, Not Avoided

Inextricably linked to thoughts about the heart is the question of emotion. It seems increasingly clear to me, the more I work with organizations (made up of people, of course), that human beings often rely on their emotional rather than rational responses to make decisions.

Of course, they look at the facts – indeed they need facts – but it is the emotional response that decides. The facts are used as a backup to the emotion.

Facts inform us.

Emotions involve us.

Emotions drive engagement, and they can also provoke disengagement. So we need to put greater effort into understanding and achieving positive emotional responses to communications. Dale Carnegie's research shows the empirical evidence for this approach.

"Analysis shows that feeling valued, confident, inspired, enthused and empowered are the key emotions that lead to engagement. Being 'valued' is the gateway to achievement ... Feeling valued and feeling confident together empower people to make decisions about their work and generates enthusiasm, which inspires people to try harder."

Dale Carnegie,
Emotional Drivers of Employee Engagement

William Kahn is widely regarded as the 'founding father' of the field of personal engagement. His extensively cited paper, published in the *Academy of Management Journal* in 1990, suggested that levels of engagement rose when "people bring in ... their personal selves during work-role performances" in terms of their cognitive, emotional and physical expression (p. 702). Kahn argued that disengagement involved the "uncoupling" of people's authentic selves from their work experiences". Thus, engagement is associated with the 'needs-satisfying' approach to motivation.

What we all know about engagement is that nobody agrees what it actually is. For example, MacLeod and Clarke (2009) stated: "There is no one agreed definition of employee engagement – during the course of this review, we have come across more than 50 definitions." Not only are definitions numerous but, more importantly, they are very different. Some definitions focus on employee behaviour (e.g. discretionary effort); some on employee attitudes (e.g. commitment); some on employee feelings (e.g. enthusiasm); some on the conditions of work and what the organization does (e.g., provides support) and some on various combinations of these. Yet others define engagement as a situation in which one of these things, such as attitudes, causes another, such as behaviour. In other words, when it comes to defining engagement, it appears that almost anything goes.

What we cannot deny is that emotion drives how people behave and perform and, therefore, the outcome that is achieved. What drives how people feel is what they are focused on or, put another way, what they are thinking. For example, take a fictitious example called Jane. Jane wakes up thinking about all the work she has to complete; her first focus is on some challenging conversations she had with her team the day before and now, as she looks out of the window, it starts to rain! She goes into work feeling grumpy, stressed and overwhelmed – how does she perform? You guessed it – not well, from the way she deals with her team to the amount of work she'll get through. Both are significantly less than normal.

Now imagine that Jane wakes up focusing on how she loves managing people, how pleased she is that she has been given some extra responsibilities that allow her to show what she's capable of – and as she looks out of the window a ray of sunshine appears! Jane goes to work energized, focused and committed – how does she perform? You guessed it – significantly higher than in the previous scenario. She deals with conflict better, is more productive and communicates better with her team.

We all know this instinctively because we all have those kinds of days. Days when our emotions drive us forward, positively and productively, and days when they don't. The key to all of them is how we feel and what we're focused on. And the same happens at work: do we focus on the negative aspect of change or the opportunities the change presents? Do we focus on our leaders' failings or on their intentions to be the best they can? Emotions drive our engagement and what drives our emotions is what we are focused on – why we feel the way we do.

Transparency is a Requirement in Modern Business

I began my working life at a time when secrecy surrounded most management decisions. That awful phrase, 'on a need-to-know basis', was rife. It demonstrated a patronizing approach that is almost shocking today.

I can hear some people saying, "It's still there, managers haven't changed that much, because knowledge is still power." That might be true, but I would argue that enlightened companies – and companies that aim to be successful in the longer term – are committed to an open, transparent management style. They know that they need to bring everyone with them to achieve their objectives, and that the ungrudging sharing of information is an essential element of a successful business operation. They realize and embrace that we live in the age of transparency – with the majority of people's lives and thoughts exposed regularly through various forms of social media.

In the age of transparency, organizations are slowly acknowledging that dull, static feedback approaches like the annual engagement survey, controlled by management, are no longer in keeping with an increasingly social-media-savvy workforce.

Due to the power of the internet, people are connecting to the things they care about more than ever. They take it for granted that they can share ideas, information and opinions across the world in real time. Given the static nature of annual engagement surveys, it's clear that the needs of employees for a real-time alternative are not being met. The world is changing, but the annual survey stays the same! While politics and entertainment and most public spaces are moving from giving people a say behind closed doors to giving them a say in public, the annual survey remains shrouded in secrecy and months of analysis.

Transparency need not simply be the sharing of information with employees through communications; it can also be the sharing of feelings with management by those employees. And if feelings are engaged in that way, more sharing happens naturally.

It's the sharing of ideas, thinking and better ways of doing things.

Being closed and secretive can be fatal to the health of a company. We know this in life; we need to adopt it in business.

"A lack of transparency results in distrust and a deep sense of insecurity."

Dalai Lama

Sharing naturally leads to conversation, our most natural way of engaging. A lack of conversation allows bad feelings to fester, causing disengagement.

People Now Expect Instant and Enjoyable Communication

We live in rapidly changing times. People have been changed by this new environment, especially in light of their evolving expectations.

One of the main drivers of this change has been technology and the increasing impact of social media. If we go back just a few years, even to the beginning of the current century, we can almost certainly remember a world without mobile phone technology, Facebook, Snapchat and Instagram, apps and all those everyday experiences that now shape our life and our attitudes.

If *you* can remember it, the chances are that a large section of the people you aim to communicate with and influence *cannot* remember – not because their memories are poor, but simply because they were not part of that world. They are Millennials, that increasingly large proportion of the workforce whose working life began after the year 2000.

But we should not be ageist. We should all try to be Millennials now. We all use mobile phones, and we all have laptops or tablets that we carry with us as central elements of our working and personal lives. And as part of that entirely natural way of living, we have daily interactions through social media, enabled by technology.

There is no chance of this changing in the near future, or even in the foreseeable future. So why have companies been so slow to acknowledge this and incorporate this new reality into their communication strategies? Can we not adapt the concision, speed and interaction of social media more effectively to the employee experience in the business world?

After all, the principles of good internal communications have applied in every age of society. The advantage of our current times is that we have figured out better means to apply them.

"Listen to everyone in your company and figure out ways to get them talking."

Sam M. Walton,
founder of Walmart, writing in 1992

The current annual engagement survey is seen as a purely 'transactional' (some might say dull) process of capturing data through a survey to support the transformational programme of engagement activities.

This is an approach I totally disagree with. It's my passionate belief that the whole process should be 'transformational'. The capturing of data must engage people and reflect how many of us already interact through social media. So no more intensive statistics-based approaches, weighed down with tick-box paper copies to reach those remote, out of the way places. And it means delivering the results to everyone, all at the same time. This is where technology can play a big part: to create a more natural and interactive experience for employees to engage with, forging a more engaging culture. So the 'survey' gives everyone a voice, harnesses what they are used to in their personal lives, fosters an engaging management style and brings the company's values to life.

Adopting this approach will mean moving away from a reliance on the statistical measurement of 'engagement', to one that views the employment experience as a dynamic, social and emotional relationship between employer and employee. To know that your 'engagement index' or 'score' has risen two points may be interesting to the leaders whose bonus is decided by it, but is almost utterly useless to the employee experience, as you can't take action to improve it because of a score.

Conversations Lead to Action

In other words, and in following Sam Walton's wise advice, we need to create the conditions for better conversations to happen. Issues get resolved through conversation; you can deal with most things by listening.

Having listened, having enabled a meaningful conversation, you can act – not simply come up with an 'action plan'. Conversations are not the same as the much-derided 'talking shop'. The point of such conversations is to explore 'why', so that you can decide 'what'. They are a faster and more certain route to a fully engaged workforce, an investment in the energy and creativity of your people.

"The best minute I spend is the one I invest in people."

Kenneth Blanchard,
The One Minute Manager

From the very moment we begin surveying, we must focus on building a conversation and environment that truly engages people, inspires them to give their best, and aligns their efforts with the needs of the business.

The survey must become the start of a conversation, where there will be natural tensions, such as time and job pressures. The conversation must be solutions-focused and about creating ideas for action – with the potential to get something done.

The conversation that happens because of what employees have said in the survey must be engaging as well. This means moving away from the 'action plan' regime – those involving lots of detailed action plans arranged within Excel spreadsheets – to one that embraces the team and company conversation as a prime source of idea generation (solutions), action (performance) and measurement. This means helping managers know how to have an effective conversation for action. We need to adopt a view that companies are effectively a network of conversations; and if this is the case, a new ability to drive engagement will emerge through conversational practice.

With more organizations being differentiated purely by the attitudes and emotions of their people, engagement has never been more critical.

The output of traditional employee surveys can often struggle in this area. It is difficult to develop an action plan off the back of largely numeric reports that contain unclear conclusions. And if we could collect employee feedback in an open, transparent and collaborative environment, participants would be able to learn and share information while the survey is open – increasing the possibility to act on what they learn. This can sharpen employees' readiness for change in that they are more aware of what people are thinking and feeling and more likely to believe that their voices have been heard.

The Result of All This

There was not necessarily one big 'eureka' moment, but rather the accumulation of a number of small eureka moments that made obvious to me the approach that would be needed. As always, I kept asking that essential question, "Why?" until I could reduce it no further. The answers to the questions were all pointing clearly in one direction.

In short, I called the idea Inpulse, for reasons that will by now be obvious. Inpulse is a way of engaging with employees in a more emotional way, having better conversations based on a commitment to absolute transparency, learning lessons and borrowing practices derived from the instant, interactive, playful advantages of social media.

"Propaganda ends where dialogue begins."

Marshall McLuhan,
Understanding Media

Inpulse is, I believe, the idea that brings an end to the era of the annual employee survey. It does so by creating an easy-to-use means to measure and drive actionable solutions for employee experience in real time which, in turn, improves and increases how engaged employees feel. It is already revolutionizing what and how many major companies are measuring as they have adopted the Inpulse approach, and I will be using them as evidence to make the case.

CHAPTER

How
Are You
Feeling?

We all have experiences that shape our careers. Those early jobs, whether they were serving pints at the local pub or shadowing a city banker, were your introductions to the world of work. What did you make of it all?

Few of us know exactly what we want to do when we move from education to paid work. It seems those days of knowing that you want to be a train driver for life are long gone. So we often stumble into our future careers, not quite sure where we're heading, but sniffing a scent of what it might be, could be, and hoping and praying it will lead to the promised land.

Starting Out

We can learn from every work experience; the failures perhaps even more so than the successes. One of my first jobs after university was as a trainee IT developer for the Your Move estate agency. Twelve months in and it was official – I was terrible at it, receiving the lowest appraisals for my work. In hindsight, it was clearly the wrong job for me; I am not a naturally left-brained person. When appraisal time came around again, with no obvious improvement in my performance, I was summoned to the office of my boss, Simon. I felt disappointed; I expected to be fired. I deserved to be fired.

To my surprise, Simon's first words were, "I'm pleased with your performance." "Really?" I asked, actually a little disappointed because I'd reconciled myself to the fact that I was not cut out to be a software developer. "Do you really think I'm good at this?"

"No, not at being a developer," Simon explained. "But your ability to make our internal clients feel good is impressive." The other departments that I dealt with were thrilled. "You listen to them, take it in, and then something happens. You sort out their problems. They know you're not technical, but you know enough to understand and to explain things simply. You phone them up and tell them how to progress. You make it an enjoyable experience to deal with IT."

This made me gulp, and it made me think: the way you leave people feeling drives so much.

By contrast, I had the example of one of my colleagues. I was in awe of his technical knowledge and ability. He was a genius developer. In many ways, he was difficult. He was morose, hard to talk to, he was sweaty and veering towards obesity. But these things were not important if he could sort out the software so easily and so efficiently, which interestingly had slowed down.

I said to him, "You seem a little grumpy."

"I am," was his grumpy reply.

"Why is that?" I asked.

"I don't enjoy working here any more; no one seems to value what I do around here and I feel I'm taken for granted."

Here was the most left-brained person I knew telling me he felt emotionally undervalued and taken for granted. And there was a clear, direct link between how he felt and the impact on his performance and ultimately (not his language) how engaged he felt.

The unmistakable conclusion that it took only common sense to draw was that it's the power of emotion that drives people and how engaged they feel.

Moving On

I moved on after a while. I had learned as much as I was going to learn and now appreciated that I wanted to apply these skills elsewhere.

Perhaps not surprisingly, I moved into human resources (HR). I know HR doesn't always live up to the humanity in its title. I remember a cartoon in which a man in line for the canteen food is raging to all and sundry – the person behind him whispers, "That's Wilkins from HR." I was determined that I would not be Wilkins. I would take this role and responsibility seriously because it is all about people, and people deserve respect. In 2004, I found myself working in the HR team of one of the biggest international insurance companies. The company was going through a period of massive change: new ownership, a big merger, complete change of leadership, and some really big decisions to be made about the future direction of the company that would involve outsourcing and redundancies.

The new leadership needed to make an announcement, and I was one of those asked to prepare the presentation that would be given to 1,500 employees. It was not going to be good news. Half of those in the audience would not be there for the next meeting in a few months' time.

We went through the 50 slides that the senior leader would present. The first one said: "Since 9/11, times have been tough." So you know things aren't going to end well! And it didn't; after that came 45 slides of unrelenting gloom and doom. That left just a couple of slides to set out what was going to happen next. It was as if a finger was going to be pointed at everyone: "You're fired!"

I was a junior in the room, with no real influence. After everyone else had given their opinions, I ventured timidly to ask, "How do we think people will feel after we've made them sit through 45 slides before we tell them what's actually changing?"

The director told me that wasn't important. "They just need the facts, the reasons we've made these decisions."

"Won't it make them even more annoyed and bitter sitting through 45 slides of justification?" It was anathema to ask such a question. These were the days before communicators talked about crafting communications based around what you want people to 'know, feel and do'. Not many years ago, but it seems like centuries in terms of attitude. A shadow had crossed their minds and a decision was made to bring in an external consultant to advise the team. I was learning how to build influence!

The consultant duly arrived, rewarded with a large prospective fee, and he sat through the same presentation. "Tell me," he said. "Imagine the CEO calls you along with the rest of the leadership team into his office at 9am. Is it good news or bad news?"

Bad, they all said in unison.

"How would you then feel to be on the receiving end of something like this – sitting through dozens of slides, knowing that your fate will be displayed on screen – eventually?" Inevitably, there was a shuffling of papers, a lot of eyes cast downwards and away, a few mumbles of, "Not best pleased. Frustrated. Angry."

"Let me put it another way: would the experience make you feel good about being part of this company?" he asked.

"So even though this is a difficult message, what about if we try to make them feel valued by the way we deliver it? Maybe tell them up front what is going to change and what it means for them personally, then maybe how you're going to help them through it and, finally, why you've chosen to do it."

Of course. You could have heard a penny drop.

Then the CIO said, "That's genius!"

I decided then, with a wry inward smile, that I would soon leave, become a consultant, get paid more and be listened to with much more respect.

The outcome was that the leadership team decided to go along with a different approach. The presentation was reduced to six slides. They explained clearly 'why' this was being done, but only after they had explained the 'what' first – and with a little more appreciation of the possible effect of the words on the audience. With some nervousness, the director stood up and presented the slides at a big theatre packed with nervous, expectant employees.

After the presentation, the first hand raised was from a union rep. Even more nervousness was evident in the room. "Should we have used the old approach? Focused more on the intellectual reasons for the change first?" He made his point in the forthright way that had put him into that role. "I'm going to fight you all the way," he declared. "But I can honestly say this is the first time we've had bad news communicated to us as if we're adults. Thank you."

This reinforced for me how powerful people's feelings can be, how we cannot afford ever to ignore the emotional reactions that people have to any experience. We are creatures of emotion; we need to be more aware of how we are feeling, to anticipate the effects where possible, and to react to them as quickly as we can. The traditional way, the best practice of the time, was to go around the offices in the days that followed, desk by desk, to gauge the temperature. Managers were advised to 'walk the talk'. The intentions were worthy, but I was convinced that the outcomes were not ideal – too slow, too subject to people saying what they thought managers wanted to hear.

Adding New Skills

I wanted to learn more. The man who had come in as a consultant was a performance coach who worked with senior teams. I was interested in what he did. I asked if I could work with him to learn. It was a risk for me – jumping off this ladder that seemed to be leading upwards in a major company, giving up a safe salary just when my wife and I were expecting our first child – but I knew I had to take it. So, I set up my own coaching company and he began coaching me on the job through the coaching 'gigs' I won.

It was a productive period for me, and I learned a lot. In particular, I learned that how you feel drives your performance. Simple, human questions opened up so many good conversations. "How did you feel when you first got this job?" I wanted people to feel emotions that were closer to that remembered experience, gaining a greater understanding of what drives the way they feel.

"What are you focused on?" became a key question.

Keep on Learning

My own focus was on a new job as an interim head of communications for one of the biggest energy companies in Europe. I had paused my own company for the opportunity to take responsibility for a team of 30 people, and this was a big step for me. Naturally, I fell in step with established practices that had been in place for several years. Prime among these was the annual engagement survey. I was excited at the prospect.

The work began five months before the survey itself was in the hands of the employees. We had to work out the messages and the questions we needed to ask. We got the number down (or was it up?) to 90 questions. After all, we had this once-a-year opportunity to engage with our people in a so-called considered way, so we felt the need to gather as much information as we possibly could. That was the decision, knowing that we would not interact in as meaningful a way with our people for the rest of the year.

The survey went out, and a lot of effort was put into making sure people completed it. At that time, in 2008, the survey could be completed in paper or online form. Once the closing date for the survey passed, it took three months to go through the mass of information so that we could report back in detail on what had emerged.

At that point, we gave the top-line results to the leadership team, with the now-accustomed 50 PowerPoint slides. The numbers didn't mean much to most of the people.

Certain numbers affected bonuses and there might be intense scrutiny over differences of a relatively tiny percentage. But none of it really affected what was happening out there in the company itself – not in the hearts and minds or experiences of the people who were contributing to performance every day. The number showing to what extent engagement had changed was the big obsession of the leadership team, because it drove another number: their bonus.

After the leadership team, the results went out to management. The questions came back: "What do you want me to do with these? I've already told you that I simply don't have the time, at least two days, to put into this exercise. And for what benefit?" The managers rightly did not want to bore their teams by simply going through the slides. They knew they needed to understand the results, interpret them, be ready to have a conversation – but they doubted that they would ever have the time for such preparations.

Action plans were expected to follow from these team meetings. We had, to be honest, fairly random numbers to indicate levels of engagement. Information was fairly higgledy-piggledy. Here it was presented as a barely digestible mass of figures, with an 'engagement number' as the outcome. But what had we learned, what should we learn, from such a number? And to top it all off, we paid a hefty six-figure fee for the privilege of this approach.

Passing Through

Fast-forward a few years – years in which very similar experiences were repeated. I was back running my own consultancy, and I was trying harder and harder to make sense of the task of the annual employee engagement survey for a number of companies. I had managed to get the number of questions down to 40 and that seemed an achievement. But there had to be a better way.

By now I was travelling a fair bit. This meant passing through airports fairly frequently, an experience that soon changed from one associated with adventure to one of tedium. You get used to those trails from terminal entrance to boarding a plane, but there was nearly always too much time spent in the airport itself, and the experience always seemed a little inhumane. You were literally in transit, connecting to a plane but not to other human beings in any meaningful way.

The introduction of buttons – one with a happy face, one with a sad face – and the invitation to 'rate your experience of security' was a sign that something might change. So you would walk through security and be frisked, have your bag searched, and wait with a degree of anxiety for it to be returned to you. The anxiety was caused by the need to catch a plane in a few minutes' time, an anxiety exacerbated by the length and slowness of the queue that you stood in. But why was this queue so much slower than the one alongside it? You noticed that the security guard on lane four was not doing his job properly; he was giving no attention to the passengers, and he was occasionally rude and caused unnecessary friction. The happy/sad face did not seem adequate as a way of rating the experience. It lacked real emotions to choose from and couldn't capture the reasons people felt the way they did.

Here was an opportunity to use instant feedback to do more than give a bland message of pleasure or displeasure. Surely there was an opportunity to go further and develop this system to highlight real problems as they were occurring – and to do something quickly to improve the customer experience. The happy/sad buttons were asking me how I was feeling, but did they truly mean it? Or was this a purely cosmetic exercise? It became obvious that you could use the system, in a much more sophisticated way, to drive performance.

Harnessing the Emotion

Something clicked inside my head at this time in 2014. We need to know how people are feeling. And we need to know at the time they are feeling it, not several months later. Why do they feel the way they do? Obviously the 'why' matters, but none of the data being collected attempts to answer that vital question in any meaningful way.

Annual surveys include verbatim comments, and these offer some of the deeper causes for engagement or disengagement. But the verbatims are too many and indigestible.

I wanted to formulate a different way of measuring how engaged people in an organization really are. To find out, at that moment of emotion, what they are really focused on. Work on algorithms suggested there was a quicker and more useful way to identify survey trends. This meant that we could highlight half a dozen representative verbatims, rather than receive an undigested mass of words. This offered the potential to do a lot more with data and to work with the emotional content of data, not simply purely factual information.

The word 'emotion' offers a clue. Remove the first letter and it becomes clearer that the role of emotion is to drive you. In every sphere of our lives – in our families, our friendships and working relationships – how we feel drives our performance. It was the reinforcement of one of the lessons from very early in my career. The power of emotion moves people to act – clearly, if we're serious about understanding, communicating with and motivating the people we work with, we need to find out more about how people are really feeling.

Along the way, I had become interested in Neuro-Linguistic Programming (NLP). It's a well-established discipline whose name suggests the elements of the approach. It's about analysing what's in our own and other people's minds through the words that are used, and seeing this as part of a system that can be used to improve the quality of communication.

I became an NLP practitioner and knew that the results I would get from interactions with people would be determined by emotions. If I knew and used this information, I could shift how people felt. Unless I knew how they were focused, I couldn't change their behaviour.

To take a very simple example, my youngest son comes in, upset at having lost at football to his older brother. I start smiling; he resists. I ask him to tell me something good that's happened. He says, "Stop it, Daddy"; he wants to be grumpy. I begin to recount a time when he realized that he could ride a bike by himself. His focus begins to change. I ask if he'd like to go for a bike ride. Smiles return.

I see this in everyday life at home. And, of course, I see it at work. The most difficult aspect of managing a team is dealing with the varied emotions that individuals feel. You recognize that diffident opening phrase: "I just feel …" and you listen not just to the factual content of the words, but to the emotions that underlie them. This allows you to understand that what they are focusing on is driving how they feel.

"To me, it has always seemed obvious that the way a workforce feels about their place of work will materially affect the performance of that organization. This is particularly relevant in service organizations, where customers are at the receiving end of good or bad attitudes. But, it is also relevant where businesses make things, or exist for other purposes."

David Smith,
Chairman of the Institute for Employment Studies
(previously on the Executive Board of Asda)

Checking for a Pulse

It was becoming clearer and clearer to me that the annual engagement survey was an event with a flawed process. We needed a better process. I began thinking with greater focus about what would eventually become Inpulse. It seemed that the potential was in every level of an organization, but that the implications were especially profound for the leadership. If companies embraced the principles that now seemed essential – understanding emotion, using real-time information, a commitment to transparency – this would even challenge the definition of leadership.

At its core it is pleasingly simple. It revolves around two questions: "How are you feeling?" and "Why?".

Perhaps one further element needed to be considered as integral. Design. I had become, as so many of us have, an enthusiastic user of Apple products. Apple has succeeded so well because they have made design as important as usage. The design relies on simplicity and intuitive use. The look and feel of Apple products are not nice-to-have cosmetic extras; they are absolutely built into the way we use the content, making it a pleasurable experience.

I wanted something as fabulous in design. And I wanted that because people have become used to using Apple's design approach; it has set the standard for the way we communicate in the contemporary workplace and beyond.

By raising the profile of listening to employees through Inpulse, I saw the opportunity to unleash the massive untapped potential for generating engagement in the attitudes, emotions and behaviours of employees. I am convinced that it is the experience of being able to voice opinions, concerns and ideas, and then be listened to, that triggers engagement.

Employees become engaged when their leaders actively seek their views in a way that can make a difference to plans and decisions. Even when not asked for their views, employees are empowered to challenge and speak out. This is not just getting employee views through an engagement questionnaire, nor is it the regular briefing group meeting run by a front-line manager for 15 or so minutes with little time for questions. It is something more profound: building a culture of participation and involvement, listening and learning.

In 2004, Dilys Robinson and her colleagues, in their book *The Drivers of Employee Engagement* (Robinson et al, 2004), identified 'the key driver' of engagement as "a sense of feeling valued and involved". This came from inclusion in decision-making; the extent to which employees feel able to voice their views; managers valuing employees' contributions; opportunities for employees to develop their jobs (i.e., have an active voice in job design and development); and the extent to which the organization is concerned for employees' health and well-being (and this means listening and responding).

By allowing employees to express an opinion, even if they think their opinions will not influence a decision, engagement grows.

In Parallel

I started to notice supporting evidence appearing everywhere I looked. All of us have had this feeling. As we begin to focus on a particular issue, our thoughts start to lead in a certain direction, and we begin to notice stories, facts and evidence coming at us from many different directions. Our minds become attuned to the subject, which has become something of an obsession. Not surprisingly, we see things as meaningful that previously might not have raised a flicker of interest. But I started collecting a wall of supporting evidence, where I could see posted statements to endorse the case for Inpulse.

For example, the four pillars enabling employee engagement, suggested by David MacLeod and Nita Clarke in their original report in 2009, included 'employee voice'. MacLeod and Clarke state that organizations with both high levels of employee engagement and high levels of performance have 'employee voice' throughout the company. Employee voice is the means by which employees are able to communicate, consult and influence decision-making, as well as raise concerns and to challenge. It allows employees to reinforce and challenge leadership views, between functions and externally.

What is employee voice? Essentially it's where an organization sees its people not as the problem, but rather as central to the solution. Employees are involved, listened to, and invited to contribute their experience, expertise and ideas. Employee voice exists when an organization has put mechanisms in place to enable it to have an ongoing conversation with its staff, in different ways, to ensure every voice is heard.

Employee voice exists when everyone in an organization feels they can have a say and that their voice is heard and listened to, and their views are taken into account when decisions are being discussed that affect them.

Many organizations in recent years have gone LEAN (creating more value for customers with fewer resources) and have incorporated continuous improvement principles into the way they work. This means that their people are empowered to redesign and simplify work processes, cutting out waste and improving customer service and the customer experience. Re-engineering business processes through employee-driven innovation has helped many organizations cut costs, grow their business, and respond to increasing customer demand, while others that have not applied these principles no longer exist.

Often employee voice is the cheapest smoke alarm you can ever install in an organization. Things often go wrong; the issue is whether you catch them before they build up to a major crisis and do significant or lasting damage. In recent times, we have all witnessed important private and public sector organizations being very badly rocked by the disclosure of issues that, if caught earlier, would have passed relatively unnoticed.

So how do you simply and easily listen to the employee voice? How do you hear not only what they are thinking, but how they are feeling about your values, purpose, vision and strategy? At a town hall where 50 or more are gathered? At the latest leadership event? After the results have been published? When they are joining the company? The list is endless, but the opportunity critical. Companies must capture how people feel about all these experiences and moments in the company life. Once you've listened and captured what is said in such a way that it leads to further conversation, then it can enable the business to adapt, shift or move as the employee voice, which includes their feelings, is heard.

It seemed that the need was unmistakeable; the direction of travel was exactly where I was heading. But first we needed to design Inpulse, make it immediately accessible and a delight to use.

"Companies instead should focus on smaller polls, where they ask about a certain issue, but on a more regular basis."

John Williams,
PwC People Management, Managing Director, 2014

"Short monthly, weekly or daily polls provide data on how their teams actually feel and catch problems before they fester."

The Wall Street Journal,
December 2014

"78% of business leaders
rate retention and
engagement as
urgent or important."

Deloitte Global Human Capital Trends, 2014

"Employee engagement
is pivotal to successful
commercial and business
performance."

Gallup, 2015

"Engaged employees give higher levels of commitment, dedication, advocacy and discretionary effort. They use their talents to their fullest and support the organization's goals and values."

Institute of Economic Studies,
Paris, 2015

"Despite overwhelming evidence that frequent measurement of employee engagement levels makes a difference, 80% of organizations still rely on the annual (or worse, the bi-annual) engagement survey to solicit employee feedback."

Jim Barnett,
CEO, Glint, in *Talent Management* and *HR Magazine*, 2015

"Companies need tools and methods that measure and capture employee feedback and sentiment on a real-time, local basis so they can continuously adjust management practices and the work environment at a local level."

Deloitte Review, 2015

"As the demographic of our workforce changes, and access to social media increases, employee research will move away from the traditional annual employee survey to more frequent and interactive research. As people become more confident in using social media, their confidence will grow in being open and honest around the way they provide feedback and comment on their employer ..."

Caroline MacDonald,
Internal Communications Lead, Hewlett Packard

"Employees' behaviour will be increasingly traceable and measurable as more information about their activity is electronically captured. Organizations will be better at studying these patterns of behaviour – in the same way that consumer behaviour is studied – so rather than asking people questions that are subject to their mood and interpretation, organizations will be using objective metrics."

Roland Burton,
Senior Communications Manager, Marks and Spencer

CHAPTER

Design
Matters

Simplicity is difficult to achieve; it requires hard work. Apple had set a benchmark in the mobile phone market, creating intuitive products that are pleasurable to use. I wanted· to use Apple and the iPhone as the inspiration for the look, feel and usage of Inpulse. In a relatively short time – think back to the mobile phones at the beginning of this century – Apple became a leader in transforming the way we communicate. This tiny device we hold in our hands now contains much of the essential data for conducting our lives, but particularly for conveying instant information about the emotions we are feeling at any given moment. Why has all this happened so quickly and, it seems, across the whole human race, in all countries and cultures, among people of every kind? Much of it has to do with design.

The technology and the software are crucial, but we should not underestimate the effect of Apple's graphics. This is design that starts from a deep analysis and understanding of how human beings might use the product.

Take your phone out of your pocket and have a detailed look at it. And if yours is not an iPhone, the likelihood still is that your phone looks the way it does because Apple set a design style and standard that other companies learned from.

If other mobile phone companies could learn from Apple, why couldn't we with the look and feel of Inpulse? It should be a tool that will be quick and enjoyable to use. People have become used to the way a mobile phone operates, so we should go with that flow; we should provide a method of use that will seem instantly familiar from this now-ubiquitous device. I wanted to achieve that 'it's just so simple' feeling in the mind of the Inpulse user.

I asked a designer named David Carroll to think about this brief. David's a brilliant graphic designer who runs his own visual communications company, but his background is in book design on the one hand (he used to be with the independent publisher Faber & Faber), and in branding on the other hand (he was a creative director at Interbrand, the world's leading brand consultancy). I thought this combination of qualities and experience would be just right for Inpulse.

I had a prototype version. David questioned me about the platform so that he could create a distinctive brand identity and a platform that would be as easy to use as possible. While David worked on these aspects, a developer and user-experience designer worked on the technical aspects to make sure everything would work as we wished.

David presented a range of options, but it seemed immediately obvious that the graphic style using triangles would be right. The triangle enabled us to show peaks (essential for the display of Inpulse's real-time information) and also troughs. These highs and lows, above and below the line, seemed to reflect the pulse of our product.

How do you feel about working for your organization?

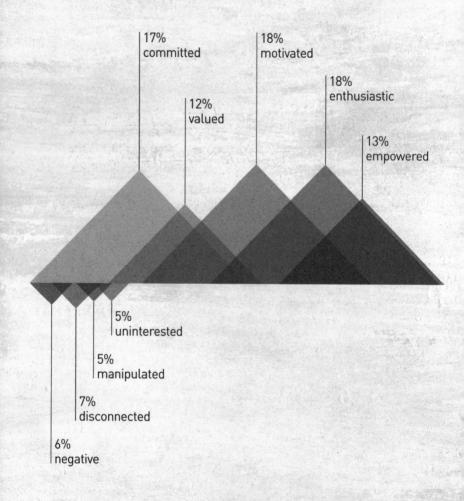

17%
committed

18%
motivated

12%
valued

18%
enthusiastic

13%
empowered

5%
uninterested

5%
manipulated

7%
disconnected

6%
negative

This worked really well for the graphic style; it meant we could display data in an instantly understandable way. To this system of peaks and troughs (see left), we could then add other graphic elements – like a word cloud and graphs – as additional means of interpreting the collected information provided by users. This worked particularly well in colour, and the colour palette suggested the range of emotional possibilities: bright colours, reds, blues, purples, greens and yellows.

"It was a little unusual, in that we decided on the graphic style first, *then* worked back to the logo and identity," David explained. "Normally it would be the other way round, but it's right in this case because ease of use was driving everything. The logo then simply echoed the graphic style so that actually it's integrated – not a case of slapping the logo on, but really making it seamlessly part of the system. With the colours and the absolutely straightforward typography, we had a strong identity, in which the logo echoed the graphic style of information communication and was a single unit rather than a separate symbol and word mark."

The pictures shown reflect the development. Overall it achieved the bright, optimistic feel I wanted. It gave us a screen for users that looked inviting, and a dashboard for us to analyse information that could be 'translated' quickly into a way of seeing that was intuitive and absolutely clear. David's stated principle was that design should not interfere with the user through the designer's ego: design everything from the user's point of view. And that was itself very much in line with Inpulse's principles of operation.

While this creative work was progressing, I had my first client for Inpulse. Of course, it was not ready in the form that I was now imagining it, but here was a client who could not wait to put the platform to use. The client was called Keith Kelly, and the company was Tracerco, an oil and gas company. The form of Inpulse that Tracerco used was, effectively, the basic prototype. Later I learned that the term Minimum Viable Product (MVP) was applied to it.

This MVP would win no design awards. It was functional and it worked well enough, but it didn't look at all exciting. It was also extremely pared down. There were only two questions: "How do you feel?" and "Why?" Keith Kelly wanted to know how employees felt about working for Tracerco, and he wanted to take regular snapshots.

Two important beliefs were corroborated by this pilot project. First, it was possible to reduce the number of questions asked of employees. Why ask 70 questions when the real nub was contained in the answers to just two? And second, closely related to that, it made sense to ask the same simple questions frequently so that you could track movement over weeks or months. This then became more evidence to argue against the traditional employee engagement survey. The honest answer to the question, "Why are we asking so many questions in the employee survey" was "because we do this survey once a year, so we need to make the most of that opportunity."

I was convinced we would get better-quality information from fewer questions asked more frequently. Tracerco seemed to prove that. It also encouraged me to think along these lines with the product that was now being properly designed. My own role in the design was less to do with graphics and technology, and more to do with content. My concern was to have the best quality of questions and the right number of questions: by 'right number' I certainly meant many fewer than the 70 or 80 that would make up the traditional employee engagement survey. And by best quality I meant that the better quality of question you ask, the better quality of answer you get. People told me they simply did not have the time to answer so many useless questions – and, if we were honest, we did not really have the time to absorb and analyse so many responses without it becoming a job-creation scheme.

"You can do it in two minutes," became my mantra, setting the objective for myself that could become a promise delivered to the participant. So this came down to only 12 questions. Twelve questions would be answered in a couple of minutes, and would gain employees' trust, as well as increase the involvement rates in the survey. If you can't find out what you need from 12 questions, you're doing something very wrong. But just two questions – as with Tracerco – was too simplistic a snapshot for many of the companies and purposes I now had in mind.

Part of the breaking down of resistance came with the persuasion that, "You can do this frequently; you don't have to limit yourself to the annual survey." More frequent use, particularly if it was easy and quick as now seemed possible, made it realistic to reduce the number of questions drastically. You don't have to save Inpulse for one occasion a year; you can use it as and when needed. As an analogy, I asked people about the quality of a relationship in which you spoke to each other only once a year – what were the chances of that ending in divorce? Or, at the very least, a total lack of understanding and breakdown in communications.

The important things to understand, in framing such questions, are fairly fundamental issues that every business needs to be clear about: Where are you heading? What are you trying to achieve? What part can your own people play in helping you get there? The business might not know the answers in detail, but it's certain that Inpulse will quickly help to get a better feel from the point of view of the leaders, line managers and all employees.

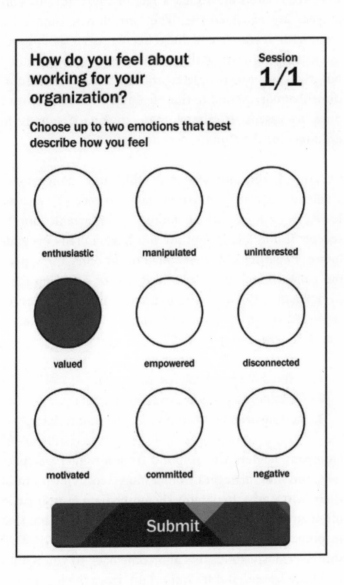

The words used are to get a feel of the emotions employees are experiencing. They are drawn from Dale Carnegie's research and have been proven as engagement triggers. Listing about 20 on each side (positive/negative), we ask people to choose five positive emotions that correspond to their feelings and four negative ones. It's essential to know these answers if you are to get a feel for the climate of your company.

Of course, this poses a leadership and management challenge. It can be uncomfortable to receive negative feedback. But it will be more uncomfortable not to receive it and suddenly find you have a crisis on your hands. Regardless of what you know or don't know, people will still feel that way and it will be affecting their performance. So, it's better to know! Inpulse enables responses to be made at different times and levels of detail. There is a three-step model:

1. Immediate response (on the spot)
2. Considered response (one week later)
3. Action-orientated response (one month later)

Company leaders will respond from a higher perspective, and line managers from a more local viewpoint of their own teams. Inevitably the immediate response can often amount to, "That's disappointing to hear", but that response will be acceptable if it's accompanied by, "We'll think seriously about this and come back to you within this time frame." But it's important, from the leadership point of view, to take concerns seriously and see them as opportunities to hold conversations that will lead to more positive feelings. From the line manager's point of view, it's best to concentrate on the circle of influence rather than the broader circle of concern. What can you influence? It might be within your team – deal with that, rather than address wider concerns. But keep in mind that the leadership needs to respond to the wider concerns, and it becomes a line management role to make sure that these issues are not swept away.

There is the potential for tricky situations, but that is the stuff of everyday work reality. What is often uncovered is that most basic and prevalent of issues: a failure to communicate well. When people cannot understand aspects of company policy, where the company is going, what it is trying to achieve – these come down to communication. From what we're learning through Inpulse, I would say 80% of problems in employee engagement have to do with communication.

In these situations, Inpulse needs to become more than just a product. If the product has identified a real problem, the vital follow-up is to understand that problem, solve it and communicate about it. Conversations have to lead to action. So the product moves from being a product to a service that is closely allied to the product. The solutions might come entirely from the leadership team thinking creatively or from within the organization. They might also come from the use of consultancies such as Quest Agency, with expertise in communications, or from other consultants with different specialist skills.

In any of these cases, the important thing is to have the honest conversation that the results have highlighted and then resolve to act where required; otherwise, the commitment to transparent engagement is undermined.

One particular example springs to mind that I will touch on in more detail in a later chapter. It seemed that a leading grocer's employees were not buying their own products, which were perceived as more expensive, even with a staff discount. This was puzzling for a company that has always had a commitment to low prices. "What's the problem? We've told them why." But the Inpulse results very clearly showed that the leadership messages had not been received via their line managers. The communication was carried out in a single session rather than a campaign. The problem could be put right through communication through the store managers over a period of time, not one communication.

As will now be apparent, the scope for Inpulse was beginning to open up. This was a vital platform, but it was much more usefully seen as one part of a service that helps companies deal with issues affecting the attitudes and behaviour of its own people. For leaders in 21st century businesses – needing to be agile, flexible and responsive – it enables better leadership. It enables a higher degree of positive engagement by all employees; engagement that is more focused on achieving the organization's own objectives and living up to a purpose that is motivating.

Using examples from leading companies that have used Inpulse, we can identify what this means in practice.

CHAPTER 4

Engaged with the Mission

The 21st century is dominated by technology. Our personal and working lives are enabled and enriched by digital technology and much of it comes in the hand-sized form of a mobile phone. At the end of the last century, such a short time ago, this would have been hard for most people to imagine.

Technology brings extraordinary benefits to us all. In the workplace it allows us to communicate instantly with colleagues on the other side of the world; it means that we can find information, understand the distinctive personality of a business, and buy products without moving from where we happen to be sitting or standing at the time. I love technology, and of course Inpulse would not be possible without it. Inpulse uses the great advantages of technology – connection, speed, accessibility, discovery – to be useful to businesses that seek just those qualities in their own business operations and communications.

Among those businesses are technology companies, many of which did not even exist last century. The giants of today's commercial world – Apple, Microsoft, Google, Facebook – have technology as their reason for being. In and among these giants are myriads of large, medium and small enterprises based around the efficient provision of technology to help keep the rest of the world functioning.

But they are not immune from the everyday issues of running a business. They need to supply services to other companies. To sell products to customers. To make money and invest in the future. To motivate and build good relationships with their own employees. In other words, they have the same need as all other kinds of companies to engage with their own people.

Perhaps technology companies even have to go further. I found myself wondering: does it become even harder to retain essential humanity and to tune into the emotions of your people as a business becomes ever more reliant on technology? Is there a temptation to use machines to communicate and forget that face-to-face communication is a human necessity? I wasn't thinking in terms of a dystopian, science fiction future, because I have faith in the combination of technology and humanity. But, at the very least, I believed that these companies must need to work hard at establishing and maintaining genuine involvement with their people.

This seemed to be borne out when tech companies became early adopters of Inpulse. Because many of these firms are necessarily security-conscious in their confidential relationships with clients, it became more difficult to name and write about them as Inpulse's clients in this book.

I'm grateful, therefore, that one such company – the awesome ARM – have allowed a short case study about its IT department.

ARM case study

ARM is a world leader in technology. Its advanced, energy-efficient processor designs are enabling the intelligence in 100 billion silicon chips and securely powering products from the sensor to the smartphone to the supercomputer.

ARM used Inpulse to gain a sense check with employees after events held for its global IT department of 500+ employees.

Natasha Liedl-McDowall, Senior Manager, Organizational Experience, organized the use of Inpulse to conduct these surveys. "Some of the key benefits of Inpulse include its ease of use in different scenarios and being able to do a survey quickly and in real time," she said.

The whole IT department is invited to these events, and a pulse check is taken country by country. It provides an insightful, enjoyable way for the IT team to feedback information on the event itself (was it useful?), on issues like the objectives and vision shared (did you understand these?), and to connect with colleagues around the world.

The feedback Natasha received from people within the department was that they liked the fact it was simple and quick to use and had immediate visible results. That's a real plus in a tech company where many people are, understandably, quite passionate about IT. They enjoyed using an interactive survey platform they could relate to and people could see the results displayed on their mobile devices, which was a key differentiator from other surveys.

The IT department also conducted four pulse checks in a year, with Inpulse helping to provide a rapid view of how people were feeling on different occasions and input as to where improvements could be made, for example streamlining processes within the team to be more efficient. Perhaps above all, it has shown the vital importance of clarity about a business's objectives. Unless you have that, unless employees feel connected to those objectives, they aren't as positive in the emotions they choose. I was excited to watch the IT leadership learning from the Inpulse results and being willing to act decisively to make changes based on feedback from the wider team.

Talking generally, technology companies have a particularly important internal audience of IT specialists. Communications can be a real issue with this group. Some people might describe them as 'geeks' but of course they are individual human beings who have a special set of skills. It's vital for a company to know how they are feeling – as important as surveying HR, Marketing, Finance or any other department.

In the summer of 2016 I met an experienced senior communications expert called Edith Wilkinson who had worked for many years in public service organizations. Edith's recent experience had been working on large technology change in the civil service and the interface between communications and technology – demonstrating the value of employee communication and bringing practices into the 21st century. Now she was working on a consultancy basis, particularly in the technology sector, through her company Artful Communication. Edith began using Inpulse and I found her observations enlightening:

"One of the key issues can be IT's reputation within the business. Sometimes IT people feel they have been promised jam tomorrow when today there are delays in delivering changes and new problems arise once services go live. The IT people can be large groups, numbering hundreds, and they can feel isolated. All sorts of underlying team issues can bubble up. The leadership team knows they are there, but don't always understand exactly what they are and more importantly what could be done to make things better."

I totally agreed with Edith that cynicism can easily develop. People feel overlooked and neglected. Perhaps this becomes even more of an issue when there is an age gap between the leadership team (who might not be tech-savvy) and the IT team (who might be sceptical about 'leadership'). Edith saw this as an opportunity to use Inpulse in such situations and to have a focus on the needs of technology companies. After all, there is a universal business imperative to be clear at the top about purpose and strategy – and to communicate this throughout a company to make sure everyone is aligned with company objectives.

Edith explains: "Companies have annual engagement surveys, so often they know that there are discrepancies in engagement levels between departments. However, as soon as they are published they are out of date. At best they give a once-a-year snapshot and that is useful to see and to record trends. I saw how Inpulse fulfilled the need for something much more rapid and responsive that can be used not just to measure engagement, but to understand it in real time."

Edith has experience of using Inpulse with CIOs in technology companies. "There can be an immediate connection, the instant ability to see potential. CIOs appreciate the real-time nature of the app and they like the idea that we can focus more on how people are feeling. They often take it upon themselves to convince the rest of the leadership team."

In common with all companies these days – not just tech companies – security requirements are a factor. But, as Inpulse works from a URL rather than being an internal system, it passes all the cyber security checks.

Edith said: "When using Inpulse I work out the set of questions to ask to find out how people are feeling about the company, its leadership and the issues it faces. It gives the information to know how to do better. The basic question, the vital one, always is, 'How do you feel about working with our company?'"

"We keep the survey open for three days, then we pull together a report. With Inpulse, the results are presented visually and shared with everyone so that vital information is not hidden away in a table or kept from employees. The graphs Inpulse produces give a clear visual representation of what is happening. All the freehand verbatim comments are shared with the leadership team, and obviously these comments remain anonymous."

"Sometimes managers can take feedback as personal but I think that's not really so. It's very clear to me that the reasons for sometimes negative emotions are due to people focusing on the processes. Management worries about 'transparency' but, if you trust your people, treat them like adults and understand how they behave in the rest of their digital life, then you will truly engage them and they will respond. People like to be asked. People like enjoyable experiences. In fact, these comments give leaders a chance to act as leaders by showing that issues raised can receive a quick and timely response. Nothing is left festering."

Word clouds are one simple and well-accepted way to see what issues are at the top of people's minds. This can point to burning issues and it can give the leadership team a huge amount of reassurance. More extensive analysis of all the data, particularly in visual form, can suggest vital areas for action. Even richer information emerges over time when trends appear from monthly surveys.

From working with Edith and other IT departments across a range of companies, including ARM, there is clear evidence that Inpulse helps identify processes that get in the way. Perhaps above all, it shows the vital importance of clarity about a business's objectives. Unless you have that, unless employees feel connected to those objectives, life is much harder. The main issue that can become obvious is the need for a renewal of the roadmap, setting out the future direction of the business, to truly engage people with the purpose and vision.

That is a need every business will recognize. With Inpulse, there is the additional advantage that you can capture ideas and information to feed into the process, and then test those ideas when they are put into action. It becomes a virtuous circle.

In short, the importance of Inpulse is not just in its ability to measure, but in its potential to help you spot issues and take remedial action.

CHAPTER

5

The Value of Involvement

Inpulse uses the technology and thinking of the 21st century. As such, many of its early adopters have come from businesses that are similarly at home with 21st-century ways of operating. Perhaps the biggest change in the way we live and work in this century can be attributed to the development of the internet. It has been a game changer for the business world, changing our approach to new thinking: transparency, the loss of deference, real-time responses and openness. All these contemporary concepts have massively impacted the way we work.

Many companies have struggled to adapt. In the retail industry, we have seen the demise of many long-established brands – BHS, for example – as well as the global growth of many brands that did not exist five years ago, let alone last century. The failure or readiness to adopt the internet and e-commerce is a major factor behind the performance of modern retail businesses.

"E-commerce is the fastest-growing retail market in Europe and North America."

Centre for Retail Research

Not surprisingly, this has had a big influence on all those issues to do with people in a business. You simply cannot sustain high levels of growth over the long term if the people who work in the business are not fully engaged and committed. This has led to much soul-searching among traditional companies, as well as fairly radical changes made by the newer ones. There are now 'Millennial' companies with Millennial workforces, and that has brought about a different mindset among employees and employers. Businesses now have young people entering employment who have no experience of 'old hierarchies', and no experience of their feelings being ignored. They are completely comfortable with mobile and online ways of working and thinking, and unwilling to put up with the delays and distancing of older management styles.

Of course, not every 21st-century company is alike, but it is instructive to look at the most successful of these companies to see how they have adopted technology, and the implications of such, into their relationships with both customers and workforces.

Peter Collyer, the People Experience Director at ASOS, recognizes that there has been a generational change: "In previous jobs I've driven the standard annual employee engagement surveys. I don't see them having a role any more, particularly in a company like this. People talk about 'Millennials' but I'm not sure if that's completely right – I see them more as 'individuals'. People joining us now are interested in 'me' but in so much as having their individuality valued in a company setting. For us the IVP (individual value proposition) makes better sense than the EVP (employee value proposition)."

ASOS is a good example of changing times – literally a Millennial business, founded in 2000. The company name originally stood for 'As Seen on Screen', but it soon became formally and legally ASOS. The company has been a phenomenal success, growing in just 17 years to become one of the world's leading retailers without a high street presence. Its customers, mainly young adults, shop online for fashion and beauty products that are fulfilled from warehouses worldwide. Starting in the UK, ASOS now sells 80,000+ products from 850 brands, as well as its own, and it does this selling entirely online. It trades in the world's major markets, including Europe, the US and China.

The growth of online retailing, driven by companies such as ASOS, is perhaps the most significant economic development of this century. The annual growth of e-commerce in developed markets in recent years has been more than 15% – the kind of growth that traditional companies can no longer dream of. Inevitably there have been management challenges brought by this fast pace, but there is evidence that Millennial companies are finding successful and different ways to manage the relationships within. The truism holds: business remains about people.

My conversations with ASOS started with its People Experience Team. It's a fast-moving company, always wanting to keep the business moving forward and with a real focus on the need to engage with its own people. Peter Collyer came into a role, People Director, that would be called Human Resources Director in a more traditional company and he has since rebranded to People Experience Team. Inpulse was then in its early development phase but it seemed there might be a good fit with the style and ethos of a company born in this century.

Discussions and intuition suggested Inpulse could be the right tool for ASOS's young workforce (they are not all 'Millennials' but their thinking is certainly 21st-century). The reality is that every generation has now taken to mobile communications; it's not confined to the younger parts of the workforce. People like mobile communication for its ease and for its ability to keep them constantly up to date. The fast pace of life and work is natural to everyone now. Which made it even more necessary to change from traditional surveys to real-time communication.

People had lost faith in the old ways of thinking about surveys. I had an impatience with it, but my impatience was reinforced by conversations at every level of the business. Companies like ASOS work in such a fast-changing sector; by the time the results of the traditional survey came out, and were analysed, a couple of months would have passed and the whole landscape shifted. The experience of Inpulse had the potential to transform that. Now there are expectations that we can have results immediately.

ASOS was on a journey that was committed to the use of online, real-time exchange. If we aimed for that with customers, obviously we had to do the same with our own people. We aimed for bottom-up communication, not top down.

"There's an important principle for me," says Peter Collyer, "that you have to treat people internally as well as you treat people externally. We need to think of the people experience not just the customer experience. This means we have to really understand what we mean by 'engagement' – it's certainly much more than having brilliant parties (even though we're great at that)."

Particularly with hindsight, it's clear that Inpulse helped bring about a different way of thinking, rather than just a change from one method to another. What ASOS discovered was that engagement needed to go much deeper; it needed to be integrated into a new way of doing things. Whereas with the old style of survey a company's leaders could agree to run a survey and then sit back without further involvement, with Inpulse there are more involved responsibilities.

With the traditional survey, you guide people with the questions you ask. You might, for example, ask a question about pay and expect a simple yes or no answer. With Inpulse, you would ask, "How do you feel?" then follow up with "Why?". This leads to much more emotional and much more honest and revealing responses, which have real implications for the way you run the business.

We discovered that we needed the senior leadership teams to lead but also to involve their own people more.

Peter tells the story of his first meeting, as a newly appointed director, with the rest of the Executive Team. He had been told 'these are our new values'. He asked who had been involved in their formulation and people looked around the room at each other to give the answer. He suggested that, as the 15th anniversary of the company was approaching, it would be a good idea to ask for the participation of the workforce.

By this point we had already conducted the first Inpulse surveys to gauge the level of employee engagement. Everyone had learned the value of taking ownership of the surveys – and thinking through the themes that would arise. It was in itself a useful way to find out how in touch each leader was with their team, and it encouraged everyone to anticipate how to deal with the issues. These Inpulse surveys got people thinking about the nine emotions that they had to pick for people to respond to – making sure there were five positive and four negative ones. The process of thinking in advance, and then planning, changed the way each leader interacted with the team.

Inpulse in ASOS had begun with a pilot scheme, choosing the biggest department (Customer Experience) first. Looking back, this was not the best choice; we should have started with a smaller department. The pilot still worked well though and now we understood many things better. We applied what we learned to surveys in other departments. The ambition was to regularly run Inpulse in each department, to take the pulse, to find out how people felt about working at ASOS and why. We asked the same core questions of each department, but were able to vary these if new questions needed to be asked about issues pertinent to a specific group.

"We were all learning," says Peter Collyer. "There is huge value in taking regular temperature checks. That first question – 'How are you feeling?' – is essential, but people's feelings are changeable. So you can't draw too firm a conclusion from one survey. What matters to me is not the individual survey but the trend. You need to do a number of Inpulse surveys to see longer-term trends emerging and we are now getting insight from that."

So, we soon had a rolling programme, with new departments coming on stream, and we were able to take into account the business's own calendar – for example, to avoid times such as holiday planning periods when everyone was manically hard at work.

When we started, we didn't think beyond the engagement survey to questions of the company's values and behaviour. Peter Collyer's arrival certainly brought that into focus as the earlier story showed: he wanted to engage the whole workforce in shaping the values, knowing that this would lead to the greatest possible embrace of them.

"I like Inpulse for its simplicity but I also want it to be more analytical at times. Using Inpulse to test the values was an indication of that, but I'm sure it could go further in the future. Inpulse can be used to measure and understand wider cultural issues, so it was useful as we embarked on a restructuring and a restatement of values. As we began the task of questioning the values, moving towards new ones, we used Inpulse to test, and then to stress test, their emotional connection for our people."

"Importantly we now see the need to use it as a more strategic tool. 'Be your best self' is now the phrase that guides ASOS and its culture. Three strategic pillars underpin this. First, how do we attract new people? Second, having recruited, how do we best equip people to do their job as well as they possibly can? Third, how do we make them feel they belong?"

The Inpulse survey of values was able to ask people about their feelings towards the proposed values. Six values had been identified. Which ones resonated most with the people? These values needed to represent the DNA of the company. Inpulse was used to listen to and involve the whole organization in what they thought but, more crucially, how they felt about each value.

How do the proposed values make you feel? You can choose two emotions.

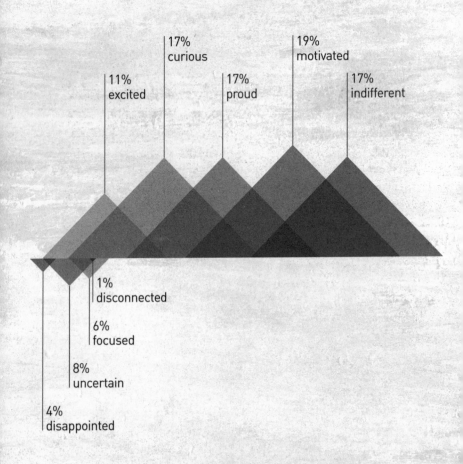

11%
excited

17%
curious

17%
proud

19%
motivated

17%
indifferent

1%
disconnected

6%
focused

8%
uncertain

4%
disappointed

The results were fascinating. Three values generated a strong positive emotional response and, because we asked why, we understood the reasons: mainly that these values were felt to reflect why people had joined ASOS and what made ASOS different. But, most importantly, because those three values helped people be their best at work. The three other proposed values didn't resonate so strongly. The company values were confirmed as: Authentic, Brave and Creative (the confirmed result also by chance had a pleasing simplicity about its ABC form).

These values are now being embedded in the business and the strategy is moving forward. Marcelo Borges has been brought in to develop the strategy. "How can we help people 'be their best self'? The reality is that greater engagement helps with all three strategic pillars: we want you to be the best professional you can. So we want people who come here to feel it was a great experience – even if they don't get the job. If you get the job, we want to help you do it as well as you can, so we'll equip you to do that – the more engaged you are, the better you'll be at the job. And our strategy beyond 2020 is about the value ASOS can bring to each individual, seeing them as unique human beings whom we want to understand. Inpulse can help us with all of that."

Marcelo sees a continuing role for Inpulse but does not wish to pin down exactly what it will be. It helps the company to listen to its own people, to link the company and individual stories to a shared sense of destiny. "What makes you proud?" was a revealing question in a recent survey.

It helps any company to understand the feelings and motivations of its own people better.

An Inpulse survey found that 75% of ASOS people had positive emotions, an extraordinarily high number. Over 600 surveys were completed within four hours, and 1,600 within days, so people are clearly valuing the mechanism itself. Marcelo talks about the data analysts on the one hand and the communication experts on the other, with Inpulse appealing to both and bridging the gap between the two approaches.

"Peter does his job from the heart," he says. "That's what ASOS aims to do. We value passion and enthusiasm more highly than skills, though of course we want both. While we can always develop skills we need people to have an innate passion."

There are challenges, of course. But the People Experience Team believe that Inpulse has a role to play in driving forward the strategies that free everyone to 'do the amazing stuff we want to do'.

"ASOS remains an entrepreneurially-led business," Peter Collyer stresses. "The founders' mentality is important. Of course the company is growing and will continue to grow, and there is a fear, felt by some, that we could become big and corporate. I don't fear that – I'd say we want everyone to be a little more professional while we work hard at keeping what we've always had. After all, we have 20 new people joining us every week. That could lead to cultural dilution but the best way to counter that is by truly understanding our people, listening to their feelings, and acting on what we hear."

With ASOS we really began to understand the potential of Inpulse. It's a very positive company that truly believes in engagement and openness. The senior team are using Inpulse to help with strategy and everyday communications. I also value their creativity because it will help to shape Inpulse's future. I always have believed in the value of creative collaboration with clients.

It works particularly well with this business that is completely at ease with 21st-century technology and thinking. Indeed, that technology is part of its strategy. Yet the basic principles of employee engagement and communication are age-old; they are all about people. Inpulse depends on, and draws strength from, its ability to bring about a better way to survey people and find out their emotional sentiment, be transparent and show the results in real time.

So, I was confident that it would work well with other companies that were older and more established and less 'Millennial' in their outlook.

CHAPTER 6

Taking the Lead

The more experiences we had with Inpulse, the more our own perceptions of it were shifting, and the more we were learning about the way organizations interacted with it. In particular, there were major issues being raised about the nature of leadership in modern business. In fact, the decision to use Inpulse is a big leadership decision for any company. It sends a signal about a company's style, and, more fundamentally, about its core beliefs, values and behaviour. It almost needs to come with a notice on the packaging: "Leadership required for best results." I have no problem with that. Much of what we do with the consultancy side of Inpulse is to coach good leaders to be better leaders.

In Inpulse, I work closely with Dominic Walters, our Director of Coaching. Dominic is a highly experienced and thoughtful coach who works directly with leaders and teams in a wide range of organizations around the world. To summarize our thinking on leadership and the role of Inpulse within it, I thought it would be useful to have a conversation with him, facilitated by John Simmons, an Inpulse associate, who asked the questions.

What are the qualities that make a good leader?

Dom Walters (DW): Leaders have to present a clear vision and then be able to explain the 'what' and the 'how' about a business, and most importantly the 'why'. Although this is only part of it, as they must be able to connect with individuals and groups about their roles in achieving that vision. They need to generate excitement about the overall picture, but recognize that detail comes further down the line. This means that they need the ability to have 'conversations with people' at every level, and this means being authentic – people won't get involved in real discussions if they think they are being played or the leader appears phoney. Authenticity builds trust and a leader cannot operate effectively without trust.

Matt Stephens (MS): I agree, particularly with the need to paint a vision. I'd also add that the leader has to set out the values and behaviours that drive him or her, to live the values and articulate those values for the company. Otherwise trust breaks down, and the leader loses the ability to influence, which is the essence of leadership.

Interestingly, Inpulse puts conversations at the heart of how the leader should respond. Classically they are used to the top-down approach of 'telling people' what has been said. With Inpulse, they have a conversation about what has been said and what it means for the team they are talking with. And a big part of the conversation is about the 'why'. But again – rather than just telling people why they are discussing it with them – learning what it means and together exploring what happens because of the 'why' – that's radical stuff!

Do you see these qualities in a lot of businesses?

DW: Unfortunately, it's rarer than you might wish. We find many leaders are strong technicians – good at the 'day job' – but often less skilled in influencing and inspiring. That said, we are all human and we all have weaknesses, as well as strengths. There is no perfect leader – our approach is to help leaders do more of what they can do well, recognize where they are weaker and find ways to manage around these. Inpulse has been interesting because it does highlight the deficiencies of a leader who is not good at engaging and communicating. That said, it doesn't take much to show them how to improve.

MS: How secure a leader feels really drives everything. Corporate life has a way of squeezing out 'good' behaviours and introducing fear. Systems and processes often militate against being that type of leader; too often the approach is driven by shareholders who are concerned primarily with financial performance. It takes bravery in a leader to 'feel the fear' and discuss the survey anyway! And especially when it's about emotions, not finances. Culture change is difficult – and globalization complicates things because companies deal with many different countries and people of different cultural backgrounds. But for any organization to thrive in the longer term, culture and behaviours must be addressed by the leader, even if that is not immediately popular. Inpulse is helping organizations deal with culture by becoming more transparent, more real time and more open to honest conversations where everyone has the same information at the same time.

More broadly, how do you think leadership has changed so far this century?

MS: Everything is faster, and the pace of change has impacted leadership styles. At the beginning of the century, there was big change every 18 months or so; now we are working with organizations that routinely face four major transformational changes in a year. Alongside this, we see new generations of workers with different expectations and who are more receptive to faster change. When I began working, just as a Millennial, I expected I would be at my employer, Aviva, for at least 20 years and the prospect of a distant pension was expected to be a vital part of the contract. Few people now see things that way. To keep good people, leaders must be in constant contact to understand their issues and respond to them. That's a big area where we have seen Inpulse help leaders, by keeping them in touch and able to have relevant conversations.

DW: I began working life a little earlier, in 1988 at Lloyds Banking Group, and recognize what Matt says – I was recruited to the management development programme and there was a clear career path. Another big change I've seen is that leadership is in the spotlight now; back then, few really talked about leadership – the boss's job was about getting the process and systems right and making sure that people did what was needed.

Out of interest, do you think management and leadership are completely separate skills?

MS: There is a big link. The language has shifted; 'management' has been downgraded as a skill and we value leadership more. Leaders can't get by with being 'just' managers. The average tenure of a CEO has shrunk – some figures say five years for FTSE 100 companies, others even shorter. There is much more pressure to get results quickly and this can't be done by only concentrating on process and things. The external pressures say 'performance is everything', we've become obsessed by performance figures; look how we scrutinize GDP figures, as well as the figures of the businesses we're part of. Leaders need to marry that with being a human being, a rounded human being we wish to follow. That's another reason why many clients value Inpulse – it enables them to connect quickly and easily into how people feel and, crucially, why they feel that way.

DW: The big difference is the 'why' question, which gives people a sense of purpose. We help leaders tap into the 'why' because that is what really influences and motivates people to give their best. It's also worth adding that 'leaders' are not always the most senior people. More and more, everyone needs to show leadership skills – helping their colleagues, supporting their teams, making connections between their work and the big picture. Sometimes this approach is formalized – for example, when organizations set up a network of local champions to support a change or new policy, they use people who have influence and that is a big part of leadership. Other times it is more informal

– we frequently help give people the tools and techniques to lead themselves and their colleagues day to day.

MS: That's true – we also help team members develop 'followership' skills. As a team member, it's not enough just to follow instructions passively, as may have been the case in the past. Strong leaders need strong followers who can give them the information and feedback they need, ask probing questions, and give constructive feedback and criticism. Leaders must create the right culture, but members of their teams need the confidence and ability to make the most of it.

Do you think there are leadership challenges facing business that are peculiar to current times?

MS: It's tougher. We are definitely seeing more expectations on leaders and greater scrutiny, hence the greater turnover at the top. We can see it in politics, too. We ask our politicians to have a view and grasp of everything – decades ago it was a much more hands-off leadership style. There is also far less deference and trust than before. The Edelman Trust Barometer, which looks at trust levels across many different countries, has shown a consistent decline in trust in leaders of all sorts. This means leaders can no longer rely on 'natural' authority. They have to work to earn trust and build relationships. We have helped leaders use Inpulse to do this – I'm thinking especially at 'key moments' or big events where top executives can use it to tap straight into what people are feeling and engage with it. For example, one of our clients ran Inpulse straight after they had been in the news for a negative reason. The very act of using In-pulse was seen as a positive decision that showed a level of vulnerability (one of the building blocks of trust), because it showed leaders were interested in people's opinions of the issue and its impact. The results were also very helpful, as they showed employees were less concerned with the issue and why this was the case.

DW: It's true that business has changed and with it so have the challenges for leaders. We used to have big, stable industries that needed to be managed – I'm thinking about the car indus-try, or coal, or manufacturing industry generally. It was about getting things made and done – meeting quotas. In many places, output is far less tangible these days than it was then. Now businesses are much more about people and facilitating the development of ideas. How they feel about work and their relationships with where they work are more important. This is one reason we developed Inpulse – to give some insight into these crucial areas that were previously tough to measure.

MS: Exactly. It wouldn't cross our minds in our business to manage people in terms of keeping strict hours and detailed planning of holiday schedules. In this new world, we all get texts at 11 at night. This makes for a difficult landscape inside corporate life and requires new skills. For example, mobile working – managing people you've never seen or met in many cases, except perhaps by a Skype call – means building a different relationship with people. Many leaders in global businesses also need to bond together a team successfully when its members are located all over the globe. It's a challenge to weave that team together.

DW: The big shift is being able to manage outcomes and outputs, rather than inputs. We have a number of client organizations that have adopted agile, or what they call 'modern working'. This puts the onus on individuals to deliver and choose how they do it. This means leaders have to shift from clock watching to creating the most productive environment for people and helping them take responsibility and flourish. That's why Inpulse is so timely – it gives insight into what people need from their work environment and helps leaders select the right levers to influence it.

MS: Don't forget the Millennial thing, too. People entering the workforce this century are less proprietorial about the business they work in, they feel less prestige about brands, less attraction to the big organization. There's no longer such big kudos to work with a particular well-known brand; there's less emotional attachment, in a sense – unless companies create that through people relationships. It's truer than ever that other people strongly influence whether individuals stay or go. If people don't get what they need, they'll move on. Our job often is to help leaders identify what it is that people do need.

DW: The old adage is true: people leave managers, not organizations. They simply decide, "That's it, I'm leaving." Funnily enough, companies have colluded in this, saying there's no such thing as a job for life. It helped them when they needed to downsize, but people have got the message and it has served to weaken the loyalty ties.

What are management looking for in leaders? What are employees looking for?

DW: Funny you say that! We've just run a number of Inpulse surveys on this very topic, asking people to say how they feel about leaders and what their most important factors are when it comes to what they want from their leaders. And believe it or not, its work-life balance. Managers feel really squeezed – there are challenges from their teams and demands from their leaders. They feel they are not getting the balance right and, therefore, need to create an environment in which they can do their best by achieving the best work/play balance. As you'd expect, vision, clarity on objectives and regular communication are all vital. But they especially need leaders to empower people to address their work-life balance – particularly in recent years, when real pay is down, workload is up and career paths are less clear.

As for employees, the Inpulse results expressed a strong desire for 'more communication'. As you look at the results, what people mean is not pump out more 'comms stuff' – they want help to think things through and a chance to clarify understanding and ask questions. We often see that line managers don't always do this well, through lack of confidence, skills or simply because they don't see the value, so they look to leaders for this.

MS: And that shows through in employees' expectations of leadership, which are many and more challenging than they used to be: "It's your job to help me make sense of

what's going on."; "Focus my actions – do my thinking.";
"Protect me from the nastiness that's going on."; "Be fair."
Along with that, there's much more emphasis on the need
to achieve something as a team, rather than as an individual. First-line leaders might express it as, "Let's do something awesome together" with much more emphasis than
ever before on 'together'.

As a result, you see teams and departments creating their
own visions, missions and values. "Don't tell me what to
do every day, let's create a framework," is what they're
saying. Within that, importantly, they're also looking for
conversations, not 'tell sessions'. Not only is the Millennial
generation much more comfortable with sharing feelings,
they expect to do it and feel frustrated if they can't. Leaders need to be good at having conversations and picking
up on feelings.

How does Inpulse fit into this new situation?

MS: Very well – as we have mentioned, it gives a 'safe' way
to talk about and understand people's emotions and have
conversations. Organizations have pushed their people to
"bring passion to work" – we have talked for years about
the need to have everyone fully engaged. There is no room
for people being half-hearted and just going through the
motions. This has let the emotions genie out of the bottle.
There is no going back – rightly – which means we need to
deal with emotions and Inpulse enables this, in a way that
leaders can deal with.

Let me be more specific. People might previously have come out saying to a colleague on their way back to their desk: "What a crap town hall." With Inpulse, we can now capture this, put figures on it, see the graphs and, most importantly, do something about it in the meeting. That creates a leadership moment – the leader can respond there and then. This can often deal with an issue and doing it can raise a leader's stature. Such an immediate response can have a real positive impact on the employee experience – they are listened to and, crucially, 'feel' listened to.

The other thing that has changed is technology. People like to express their emotions, views and opinions through social media, most frequently using mobile phones. We've gone way past the situation where the primary purpose of a mobile phone was to talk to someone voice-to-voice. A phone now enables emotional expression. Inpulse plays easily into that situation. It's the right platform for exploring a wide range of issues.

DW: Leaders are effectively saying – to everyone they lead – "We want you to have a relationship with us, to align your emotional energy with ours." They are committed, as part of that, to being transparent and authentic, and to having conversations that involve all parts of a business. Inpulse fits that agenda and situation completely.

Leadership moments sound like they demand bravery and an equal display of emotional engagement.

DW: They do – but they are very important. Employees – even that term seems outdated – see them as a sign of the more dynamic relationship they seek: "Let's create something together." In a meeting, no one can hide any longer: there is that leadership moment, an opportunity that comes often out of a difficulty, out of adversity. Think of Princess Di's death – that was a leadership moment for Tony Blair, an opportunity to speak for everyone and bind us together. His response helped define how people saw him, until it was reshaped by other, less successful, leadership moments. There are micro equivalents of that in companies all the time, and leaders need to recognize them as an opportunity, not a threat. Borrowing an example much closer to home for most of us, think of your relationship with your partner – that demands openness, transparency and emotional commitment. We assess its health by how our partners respond at key moments.

MS: I see these as moments of truth – opportunities to truly demonstrate leadership. The challenge for the leader is that this is transparency in action. Questions are asked, people respond with emotional honesty and the results are shown instantly.

The leader must respond on the spot from a gut feeling, to deal with a difficult issue that arises, to have a further conversation, to talk and do something. In the past, the aim might have been to close that issue, effectively to kick it into the long grass. That isn't acceptable now. So Inpulse offers the positive opportunity to respond with a leader's own moment of truth. With the old style of employee engagement survey, the best that might have happened is that there would be a response weeks or months down the line.

So the brave leader at the top tier has to deal with this. Many leaders have become socialized to the old way of doing things, so they don't instinctively know how to respond. Of course, it's understandable that they might feel exposed when they see comments displayed, but by handling them well, leaders can turn things around and make a positive out of a negative. We often coach leaders to make the most of these moments of truth. They can have a real discussion about how these issues can be resolved, and it's much more likely that something will happen. It's far more involving than an old-fashioned action plan produced months later with little involvement of the 'staff'.

How will Inpulse support good leadership?

MS: We have seen that conversation is the key to building relationships with people. With Inpulse, the evidence is instantly available – there's no need for number-crunching delays – so leaders can start talking. Often, the very act of having a conversation can help resolve the issues – people just want to know they've been heard. If the matter goes deeper, then the conversation can lead to a resolution. Inpulse gives discussions real substance and focus. It stops them from becoming frustrating 'talking shops' that lead nowhere. Often, discussions lead nowhere because they end up concentrating on what Stephen Covey described as the 'Circle of Concern' – those issues that bug us but are outside our influence. Too much of this makes us feel impotent. Inpulse helps conversations focus instead on the 'Circle of Influence' – those issues or aspects of issues about which we can do something. This makes for much more productive and rewarding conversations.

Inpulse highlights where a leader can focus time and energies best, to turn attention to where they can have most impact. Insights are clearly shown, and you should take advantage of that clarity to take some steps that will prevent negativity festering. Now that it's out, deal with it and move on.

DW: We know that the employee experience matters, which means that measuring it matters, too. Listening, responding, being open, accessible and consistent all help create a culture of trust. Trust is the most valuable asset for any leader, in any organization. Inpulse provides a way to measure employee experience and have the right conversations about it. It answers the need in people to be heard and for that to lead to something.

MS: It's a way to manage the genie, to manage emotion. But, of course, it's not something you can use every day, you have to be selective and plan it. Inpulse is, in its essence, very simple and elegant while hiding the detail of analysis. It tries to get back to absolute simplicity. It avoids the over analysis that can lead to paralysis. Let me give you an example; our algorithm for free text questions goes through every response and then chooses the top five most representative across all the responses. This is huge, as it saves managers and leaders hours of reading – not to say they don't need to read through all the responses, but in the moment they can see the most representative responses and it gives a clear steer as to what people are thinking. The feedback on this feature has been huge, as managers value the time it saves them – simple and effective.

Simplicity is important for another reason – people are more likely to respond to Inpulse because it is short, but also it makes it manageable for leaders. That's why we put a limit of 12 on the number of questions. Any more questions bring rapidly diminishing returns. Besides, the big 60 or more questions on surveys of old were often driven by their lack of frequency. Because Inpulse can be used regularly, it can be more targeted and precise and people feel like they have a voice that is heard.

So, leadership and Inpulse – what are our conclusions?

DW: For me, this discussion has reinforced that leadership is more crucial than ever and the importance of the ability to give people purpose, and create the environment in which they can achieve it. Running through all this is having open, regular and meaningful conversations that build trust. That is where Inpulse can be so powerful – providing a simple and effective way to highlight issues and focus these conversations so they achieve something.

MS: A key point for me is the importance of leadership moments – opportunities for leaders to connect with people, and to demonstrate leadership by addressing issues and tackling them in the moment. Inpulse enables these moments by providing instant insight on what's on people's minds so it can be addressed. Overall, though, it's clear that there have been massive changes for leaders, with much more to come. And interestingly, Inpulse is not only helping leaders deal with these changes, it's speeding up the changes happening within leadership: transparency, regular communication in real time about what people are thinking and feeling, and enabling the employee voice to influence decisions. It provides a usable, robust and credible connection between people and their leaders. It helps them be heard and feel they are being heard about things that matter to them. This will build and sustain trust, which is rapidly becoming the essential resource for successful leaders.

CHAPTER 7

Flexibility
in Time

There's always the temptation to tell a story with a beginning, a middle and an end. By the last page everything is resolved, and the hero rides off into the sunset. Of course, it's tempting, but it doesn't necessarily reflect real life. Most real-life stories turn into multiple tales. One story leads to another. There's a continuing thread, so you never quite reach the point where you can say, "There, it's done. The end."

I suspect the story of Inpulse and Time Inc. is like that, but I think this makes it all the more interesting and more real. We can drop into the story as it was at the end of 2016, knowing full well that the narrative will unfold further and develop in interesting ways in the years ahead.

This is a story of change management, and the situation is very much about the changes facing most companies in the 21st century. These changes were brought on by technology, leading to new ways of working inside a business and relating to customers outside. Time Inc., the well-known US corporation based around the international *Time* business magazine, acquired the UK company IPC Magazines in 2001. No major changes were instituted, but in 2007 the company bought a building (Blue Fin) in Bankside, near Tate Modern, perhaps an indicator in itself that the company needed to reflect changing times. A few thousand staff were employed, producing magazines that are household names, and they occupied most of the 10-storey building.

But times were changing (it's almost impossible to write about Time Inc. without unintended puns arising).

Increasingly, the owners realized that they had a print business operating in a digital world. Sales of printed magazines were falling, readerships dropping, advertising declining. Advertising – so important for magazines – was changing because of the presence of Facebook, Twitter and other new media. Customers and readers were finding new ways to forge relationships with their interests and hobbies that were previously based around specialist magazines.

The range of such magazines was extremely wide, catering for interests of all kinds: *The Field, Marie Claire, Angler's World* and *NME* are a few examples. Of course, the company responded to the changing environment. If it had not, it would not be in business today. In 2013, the UK company was renamed Time Inc. UK, and soon after a new CEO, Marcus Rich, came in to transform the company into a modern multimedia business. By this point, magazines had been withdrawing from print and moving to web-only versions. There were some 60 of these magazines, powerful sub-brands in their own right, with greater brand loyalty among their individual readers than the parent brand could command.

NME was an interesting case in point. *NME* (*New Musical Express*) was a music magazine that had been the leading source of news about popular music and artists for many decades. It had been around before the days of The Beatles, introducing the first singles chart in 1952, and had attracted and developed young writers and editors like Julie Birchill, Paul Morley and Tony Parsons. It had established a high standard for music journalism in print.

Perhaps music in the modern world would not have grown to be the force it is now without *NME*. But, in this century, its print sales were in steep decline, and the magazine moved to a digital version – which became the most visited music website in the world. Interestingly, *NME* lives on in a print version that is handed out free to encourage greater traffic to the website, where music videos have their natural place, attracting young music fans. So *NME*, and Time Inc. generally, adapted to the changing situation.

Time Inc. has a new strategy in place, achieving growth organically and through acquisition. The focus is on areas of strength such as cycling, crafts, fashion and beauty, and equestrian, but the online presence is always dominant. Classified advertising – that had been the main attraction to readers of many of these magazines – has adapted and incorporated the visual techniques made possible by technology.

But what about the employees? These were enormous upheavals to process in terms of ways of working. Not surprisingly, there was turbulence because this is – by professional requirement – an informed, opinionated, articulate workforce. No wonder, as someone put it to me, some of the new leaders were wary of being asked awkward questions by experienced print journalists (the term 'wizened hacks' was used fondly and ironically).

Time Inc. invited Inpulse in to work with the HR team on internal communications: to assess the situation, make recommendations and develop a communications plan.

The team was headed by HR Director Lesley Swarbrick, and Paul Phillips led the internal communications. It was an intelligent, experienced team, but they had been riding a rollercoaster in recent years, not necessarily with the best equipment for that task. There were surveys, largely qualitative and driven from the United States, that 'didn't land well'. The top 120 leaders were saying the right things, but staff found it difficult to understand what was going on with the business that they were an integral part of.

Lesley instituted 'Let's talk', a series of town halls where leaders would give updates and answer questions, as a signal of intent. As part of the communications plan devised in partnership between Time Inc. and Inpulse, we all recognized the need to engage more effectively with people. Minds were concentrated all the more when, at the end of 2015, Time Inc. sold the Blue Fin building to create funds to invest in the future of the business. Part of the business moved outside London to Farnborough; plans were drawn up to relocate most of the rest of the business, leaving just one floor (out of ten) that would remain for the advertising department (which needed to be near central London's media activities). In the meantime, hot-desking became the new norm of everyday working life. An extraordinary amount of change happened in just a couple of years, and it seemed to be accelerating.

"We recognized," explains Paul Phillips, "that internal communications was a critical issue. And it was an issue we were determined to improve. Messages were fed down, but there was a hiatus, the messages didn't percolate.

The editorial teams, for example, were being asked to work in totally new ways – amalgamated editorial teams between previously separate magazines – and levels of cynicism were high. You only had to talk to people, as we did, to find a large degree of resentment and dissatisfaction. Our conversations with Inpulse explored a number of options, and the Inpulse platform was part of the conversation."

Lesley Swarbrick put it like this: "The Inpulse platform was quick. It was on your phone and easy to use. The way it looked, working visually, was an attraction in an organization that made its living from conveying information in words and pictures. Ease of use, speed of data explanation, the power of the visuals – these were attractive to us. Also the fact that, for a user on the team, it almost became a prize that you could see the results before your eyes in a completely transparent way. That offered the opportunity to build trust and break down cynicism."

Paul Phillips continues: "Our need was to communicate change, and to communicate the need for continuing change. Change was the new reality. Unfortunately, there were cost-cutting actions, some redundancies, the loss of more than 500 staff compared to three years earlier, and the greater use of freelancers. But the aim was to invest money for the future of the business. Not necessarily the easiest message to communicate, but that was where we were."

How do you feel about working at Time Inc. UK?

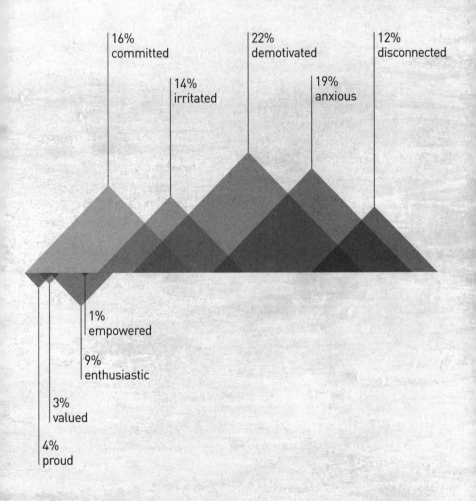

16%
committed

22%
demotivated

12%
disconnected

14%
irritated

19%
anxious

1%
empowered

9%
enthusiastic

3%
valued

4%
proud

The first Inpulse survey was in October following the announcements about the changes delivered by managers. As always, "How do you feel?" was the lead question. Results from the first pulse survey highlighted high levels of negative emotions that were causing disengagement. The reason was fascinating. Very clearly people who chose the negative emotions explained that their reason for doing so was because they couldn't see where Time Inc. UK was going and, therefore, what the future might look like for them personally – rather understandable why they chose emotions such as worried and fearful.

Of course, the plan introduced more than just Inpulse, and within weeks of that first use there was an event at the Hilton (taking people off-site) at which the CEO set out the strategy, backed up by people at stalls giving information and answering questions. We ran Inpulse to test the reactions during that day, and this gave us really valuable insights into people's levels of understanding and engagement. This second survey a month later gave us valuable insight into the emotional journey of employees. After being face-to-face with the CEO and hearing about the future, they chose positive emotions like 'hopeful' and 'excited'. Yet when the same message had been delivered by managers a month earlier, there was a negative response. Interestingly, we could see the reasons why and where there were differences between different departments.

The first survey showed that cynicism was high precisely because people didn't feel that they were being given a clear picture of what the future would look like, and, therefore, their place in Time Inc. didn't feel secure. Positive emotions rose considerably after the event, which had provided the opportunity to hear directly from the CEO what the future would look like and question the news face-to-face. Seeing the results – to which they were contributing – on a big screen in front of them helped to break down barriers; people liked the transparency, and they liked the anonymity of the survey (something we stressed as vital).

We decided to run a pulse survey, to test the temperature a month after the event. This time the response level rose above 50%, so there were positive signs that people were accepting the medium more (and, of course, that response rate was higher than more traditional survey methods). The results were still not an overall good reading for the leadership team. Employees were not as engaged as the leaders would have wished; they were anxious about their positions and about the future.

How do you feel about the changes announced last week?

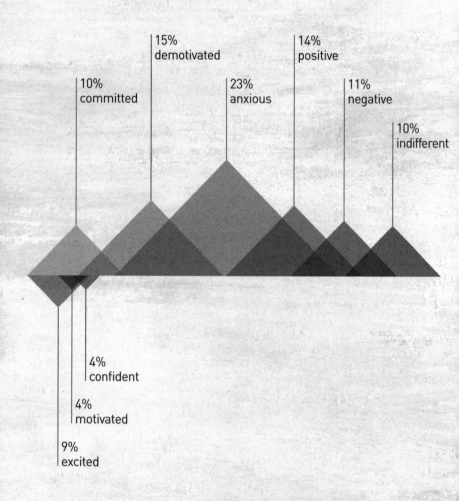

10% committed

15% demotivated

23% anxious

14% positive

11% negative

10% indifferent

4% confident

4% motivated

9% excited

"That wasn't disappointing," says Lesley. "That was what we expected, given the situation we were in and what people had been through. What was valuable was that it gave people a voice, enabling conversations that didn't exist before. For me, there was great value in having my intuition validated. Here was the evidence; it couldn't be avoided. In fact, this meant we could all share in the situation and, importantly, start taking some actions that addressed the issues raised. I found it particularly helpful to have easy access to the most representative verbatim but anonymous comments recorded. There was a real commitment to transparency and that, as part of an ongoing programme, puts us on a better path."

Inpulse had revealed some big moments of truth. First, that Marcus the CEO was a good communicator who could clearly articulate the future. Second, when employees heard and were able to question the strategic direction and future of Time Inc. properly (at the event with the CEO), they were highly likely to be engaged by it and show positive emotion. But most importantly, where it was left to managers to communicate the message, if they didn't feel briefed and weren't good at communicating, the message failed to land and was having a massive impact on how people felt and, therefore, how they engaged with the changes happening. This was having a big business impact, as Lesley knew that the changes weren't happening as fast as they needed. Not surprisingly, when people weren't engaged with it, this slowed down the business transformation needed to help the business succeed. As a result, Lesley asked Inpulse to deliver a programme to upskill managers on communication. She also asked Inpulse to work with the executive team to develop the business narrative to capture in a simple format what the changes were in a way that could be communicated simply and powerfully – through stories. Inpulse was driving real business change and shaping how the leadership responded to the impact of the changes.

Lesley talks about transformation, about this being a transformation journey for Time Inc. She has a broad vision and rightly sees that Inpulse is only one piece in the toolkit that is needed to bring about real change. Yet she also identifies Inpulse as critical to that direction: "How else could we track progress and gather insight better?"

Inpulse is now integral to their internal communications programme. In 2017 we will run quarterly surveys, which will come after half the managers have been through the communication coaching, and more are scheduled through the year. There is a very practical dimension to the next survey, because the office move will have happened – teams will have moved from the Blue Fin building to Marsh Wall and other locations in the period just before Christmas. The survey will give a sense of how the move has gone and will start to identify trends in peoples' attitudes (for better or worse). The story continues, as I wrote at the beginning of the chapter.

"With change, there's always bad news," says Paul. "There will, inevitably, be more in the new year. But we all need to get used to the fact that change is a constant. Certainly for Time Inc., and I suspect for most other companies. In the long run, we will become a more focused, more democratic company."

While maintaining the commitment to anonymity, there are segmentation conclusions to be analysed, and these are a challenge to the leadership rather than the staff. If a department is shown to be lagging in its understanding of the strategy, it reflects on the way that department leader communicates. That is understood and accepted. There is no punishment attached. Time Inc. operates with a carrot rather than stick approach. Accompanying this programme are new coaching sessions to equip leaders to communicate more openly and effectively with their teams. Inpulse's value is in flagging where there are issues and enabling those issues to be addressed with supportive action.

"Why are you disengaged?" asks Lesley. "Is the problem attitudinal? Is it not seen as your role to communicate? We have brought in a new way of working and it won't go away, so here is support to help you. Inpulse then gives us the means to monitor how effective we are in bringing about this change of culture.

"Inpulse immediately felt completely natural in today's business environment. As if it should already have been there. Its simplicity and ease of use make it crucial for a business on a transformation journey. It helps us measure what we're doing, tailor resources and messaging, and engage far more effectively with people. It's simple, but sophisticated.

"So we will use it in the future as an essential element of what we do. We will integrate it into events; there are a lot of tailored ways in which we could use it. The only issue, for me, is wanting to keep it special, not to overuse it, because it has such power and I don't want to dilute it. I want it to be associated with the culture change. Because there's no doubt that it creates a sense that we are 'together'; it brings a sense of connection to everyone working in the company."

Of course, there is a correlation between engagement levels and the quality of briefing, so Inpulse becomes an instrument of improvement. It cannot in itself make poor communicators into good ones, but it can point out where help might be needed. In parallel with Inpulse, a new system has been introduced, called Communication Champions, people who are identified as having good skills and connections to the grass roots of the business. As a result, many more effective conversations are taking place, and those conversations lead to a shift in attitude. Feedback still shows that cynicism is prevalent, but that is partly human nature and partly the need to allow the effects of time to work through the system. In a sense, the change of location is a visible demonstration of change that can be helpful.

Inpulse is not only integral to internal communications – part of the way Time Inc. has chosen to measure progress – but it is also helping to shape business decisions, like the leadership team clarifying the 'story' of change and rolling that story out across the organization. New initiatives happen as a result of feedback from Inpulse surveys, and there is a better system of informal communication – simply better conversations – between surveys. Inpulse has been particularly successful in demonstrating the importance of face-to-face communication at every level of the business.

For Paul Phillips, first trained as a man of words, a magazine journalist turned internal communications manager, it has had another surprising effect: "My own written communications have changed. I now write in a different tone of voice. Before it had been too formal, too corporate-speak, sometimes patronizing, often long-winded. Inpulse has made me more aware of that. I now adjust my local messages to be more informal and concise, and I have found that liberating."

The Time Inc. story has had an effect on me, too, by making me more aware of Inpulse's potential. I like the flexibility that Time Inc. brings to their use of Inpulse – and I had always hoped that Inpulse would be flexible. But I particularly like such flexibility because it opens up countless avenues for further development and for new stories to be shaped by Inpulse in the future. I'm a great believer in collaborative partnership, and that describes the way we are now working.

It's also worth noting that we used Inpulse to measure the impact of the communications coaching programme. Having feedback available instantly from the Inpulse survey, we could see straightaway how people felt and had an aggregated picture of their responses. It allowed us to have productive conversations with the client while things were fresh in our minds on how to evolve the programme so that the following day's coaching programme reflected the feedback.

Secondly, it was really helpful to have a clear understanding of how people felt as a result of the workshops. In the past, we have seen coaching appraisals that ask questions about, for example, how useful coaching has been, its impact on people's skills and relevance to the challenges they face. These are all questions that give helpful information about the impact of a development programme, but understanding how people feel gave a strong and clear picture of what people were taking away from the coaching.

A founding principle of Inpulse is that the way we feel impacts what we do which, in turn, influences the results we get. Being able to tell how people are feeling after coaching really gives a strong indication of how successful it has been and how likely they are to put what they have learned into practice. We were delighted that 86% of the responses showed positive emotions of engagement, which showed that people were leaving motivated, excited and confident. We were also able to see that 14% still felt anxious, uncertain or irritated, which will help us refine our content for future workshops and make sure we allow more time for reflection and for people to raise issues.

Our response to these more negative emotions was also interesting. When we are working with clients, we often caution them against focusing too much on the minority emotions, whether positive or negatively expressed and to focus on the dominant emotions. We found ourselves doing it, though, and had to challenge each other to put the minority of negative emotions into perspective. It was a useful reminder for us of how leaders and others who are receiving comments on things in which they have a strong emotional investment are far more likely to give undue weight to the downsides – and the importance for us as facilitators and coaches of ensuring they keep a balanced view.

Thirdly, we found the free text comments and reasons why people had responded as they did helpful. Often on feedback forms, people do not give comments or, if they do, write long pieces. Because open responses on Inpulse are restricted in length, however, we found that more people responded and what they said was more to the point and easier to understand. We had some very useful steers on what was working well and suggestions for making the workshops even more powerful. In all, a useful experience not only to get quick, powerful and practical feedback, but also a good way to model to clients how to respond to and do more with what Inpulse tells them.

This story does not end here. It ends only in the sense that we have reached a certain moment in time, and I am writing about it from that moment. Even as I do so, I am aware that the most interesting stories are yet to come. As with any good story, I look forward to finding out what happens next, and who the new characters in the story will be.

Anticipating the Sea Change

When you survey the landscape of great brands in the industrial history of the last 100-plus years, there are not many names more famous than Rolls-Royce. For once the term 'iconic' seems completely right. It's a brand that stands for an extremely high standard of engineering based around many different forms of transport, including cars, planes and boats.

It was exciting to be contacted by Rolls-Royce Commercial Marine. This was a company that could rightly claim to be world leader in vessel design, extending into offshore oil and gas rigs. With 25,000 commercial vessels using Rolls-Royce Commercial Marine equipment, 3,600 employees located in more than 30 countries and revenues of £1 billion, this was a significant business. But it was a business that had been put up for sale.

People sometimes liken the process of selling a business to selling a house, as if to reassure you that it's all quite normal. It may be, but I've never found the buying and selling of houses devoid of stress. So, it is understandable that employees in a business that is being sold will feel some anxiety. In fact, many emotions are involved.

Kim Kersey, who had been HR director at Rolls-Royce Commercial Marine since 2015, was part of the senior team behind a deep-reaching programme of change. A strategic review was led by the division's president, Mikael Makinen. The company's footprint had been halved – there had been a 40% reduction in the workforce – but there had also been a significant cultural shift following the review. Change is often painful, but here people felt this was a much better place to be. There was a commitment to a more open, transparent style of leadership and this was working.

In discussing organizational development with another HR director, Kim heard about Inpulse and decided to find out more. When I met her, I was impressed by the cultural change that was already happening. The role that Inpulse could play was not to initiate such change but to support it. This was an interesting starting point.

What Rolls-Royce Commercial Marine was looking for was a simple, agile way to get regular employee opinions. Previously, they had relied on traditional survey methods, and these had deficiencies that I knew well. A lot of effort had gone into an annual survey that gathered a great amount of data that then needed to be analysed. The data went up to the CEO and then, in time, was cascaded down to employees. The process took many months and the main problem was that it was seen as the senior leadership's information.

Kim was looking for transparency that would achieve greater ownership of the information, and of the resulting action plans, by all employees. If directed well, it could provide a focus for leadership learning, linking to the strategic review that had initiated the cultural changes. She wanted something that would go with the flow of a more rapid and receptive leadership style, with a real commitment to listening to the whole range of people and nurturing richer, more meaningful conversations.

Kim believed Inpulse would help deliver that, moving from previous surveys that captured one moment in time to a new approach of continuous listening and conversation. Inpulse would help move away from a paper-based, traditional computer setup to the mobile technology that can now reach everyone, literally putting the means into everyone's hand. In doing so we could move from long, complex surveys that needed exhausting analysis to short, focused, instant results with insights that made an immediate impact.

The technology would be important, but this was about much more than just technology. It would be about developing leaders, inspiring communications, shaping culture. Kim tells the story:

"The first time we did it, Mikael called me to say he'd filled in the survey and had then sat mesmerized by watching results happening before his eyes. It really set off a buzz through the organization because it was clear – there in front of you – that the data was for everyone, not just for the leadership."

The Inpulse campaign unfolded in three phases. First, in April 2018, there was a 'pulse check'. The results were encouraging: 2,356 responses amounted to 67% engagement. We knew from this that there was a mixture of curiosity and optimism, as well as quite high levels of anxiety. The word cloud revealed that there was, above all else, a hunger for more information.

As a result, we decided that we needed the next survey to focus on the leaders. And so, we undertook a 'deep dive'. From this, with 79% engagement by the group, we knew that we had to provide leaders with more support to help them lead bold change; they needed information and opportunities to inspire and impact.

Meanwhile, the sale was progressing and the Norwegian company Kongsberg had emerged as the buyer. We wanted to know from everyone: "How do you feel about this?" So, it was agreed that a further pulse check survey would be run.

Let me pause here to reflect on this with you. It's easy, in retrospect, to get caught up with the momentum of a story and to lose some of its emotional significance. Conducting this next survey was a BIG decision and a very brave one. Imagine if the pulse survey had shown – and it would be impossible to hide because the results were immediately visible – that there was a very negative reaction to the purchase among employees. That would leave the leadership team with a major problem. The stakes were raised even higher when Rolls-Royce Commercial Marine said that it would share the employee survey results with Kongsberg. The risk was evident – it was quite a large risk – and it was important to face that bravely. That is what the leadership team did, and it proved to be quite helpful.

"Of course, there were some anxious moments in advance, but there were also some laughs along the way," said Kim. "When we were designing the questions, we were trying to identify nine emotions that would translate easily into Finnish and Chinese. There seemed to be no big problems with all the other languages but you can imagine that Mikael, as a Finn, received some teasing about the absence of emotional words – and perhaps emotions – in his native country. He laughed with us.

"The results were positive, perhaps more so than we had expected. It was good to have the hard data – and a bonus that we could share this with Kongsberg – but it was also noticeable how the values behind Inpulse were now chiming with the cultural transformation that was taking place across the business. I observed leaders in team meetings opening conversations with, "How do you feel?" The emotional trigger behind Inpulse was coming out not just in the survey itself, but in other interactions as well.

"Much of this was down to the quality of the questions in the Inpulse survey," she said. "I learned the importance of getting these questions right, and Matt was always a good guide. Questions that started with, 'How were the leaders feeling' went on to ask, 'How much energy do you have now' and 'How do you feel about the future'. Some of those questions were deliberately tough but, for example, asking about energy levels was a useful recognition that everyone had been going through a tough, draining experience with the process of sale and transition.

"As a result, we used Inpulse for more than 70 people in the MLT (Marine Leadership Team), who would meet twice a year. We could use Inpulse to discover and discuss what they were feeling and how to support them in their roles. And, it could serve as a signal to take proper accountability.

"Of course, the results were not uniform across the business, but that became another useful aspect of Inpulse. We could see a whole company picture, and we could also easily analyse information by particular sites and countries. There were regional variations – for example, showing a more positive response among the Nordic companies to Kongsberg. That was not unexpected, perhaps, but useful to feed into communications. It was particularly helpful in shaping communications for some of the regions that seemed more fearful of what was happening. There were hotspots that were easy to spot.

"So," Kim said, "if you could see lower results in, say, Brazil or China or Korea, it became possible to arrange special communications for places identified in this way. Mikael did a number of webinars 'just to get closer to the people' and these were important in building trust."

The results were there to see, but they were not just evidence of the impact of Inpulse. They were about integrating Inpulse into a broader communication plan. The surveys gave greater impetus to the direction in which the company had been moving, building on the hard work that had been put in over the previous couple of years.

It's always important to see the connections, and perhaps Inpulse has a particular value in making those connections more apparent. Knowing what was on people's minds – in response to that simple question, "How do you feel about the business?" – led to other positive things. For example, it led to the production of a Rolls-Royce Commercial Marine book that told the company story and built a great sense of pride. Everyone got a copy of that book, and it contained many of the verbatim comments from Inpulse surveys. We could also use the word clouds to focus on what gave people most pride and pleasure from their work, which helped both acknowledge and celebrate the company's people.

"Transition starts with an ending," said Kim. "You have to manage the process. Inpulse played a vital role in helping us through the transition, to an effective handover from one business to another. It helped people embrace the future."

So, now a different business situation is in place. Two businesses have become one, and they inevitably retain some aspects of their own, different cultures. No one would expect anything else. But Kongsberg is aware that the strength of Rolls-Royce Commercial Marine's culture is a positive factor that they need to embrace in the new company.

Here are some final thoughts from Kim: "Inpulse brings a healthy and essential focus on emotion – that's its starting point and its unique point of difference from other kinds of surveys. It's extremely agile, which goes with the ability to run it frequently for best effects – the annual survey seems very outmoded as a result. But it brings things alive because it's not just a survey and it's not just about data.

It helps a company think through those fundamental questions, particularly, 'Why do we do what we do'?

"It enables you to support leaders better and to develop more targeted, effective communications. There are not just facts; the depth of insight helps make meaningful interventions possible. I was particularly taken with the 'boot camps' that emerged. These experiments helped leaders to tell their own personal stories and to realize that these made powerful connections with their teams. Although 'boot camps' sounded military, they were not like that. It was about enabling people, getting them ready to face the future. And I'm convinced that the approach demonstrated by initiatives such as these, with the involvement of innovations like Inpulse, will be a vital part of the future. Such developments are critical as we deal with change."

From my point of view these are encouraging words that provide a lot of food for thought. What does the future hold for companies in the 21st century? One thing seems clear: there will be more information, and a greater need to use that information well. That's a big challenge for every business. The recurring 'emotional word' throughout the Inpulse surveys for Rolls-Royce Commercial Marine was 'curiosity'. It became clear that employees had a real curiosity about what was happening in the business, and where it all might lead.

I see no likelihood of companies, and their employees, feeling any lessening of curiosity in the future. This will lead to greater engagement. And that gives me great hope.

CHAPTER

9

The
Revolution
Continues

We live in a changing world, and one of the things that is changing most rapidly is the working environment. By that I don't mean bricks and mortar, the spaces in which we work – though they are inevitably changing, too – but the context in which managers manage, leaders lead and 'employees' think about their workplace and work more generally. The spaces inside people's heads and hearts are very different from their equivalents in the previous century. What are they actually feeling at any given moment in a business's development? Do you know? Shouldn't you know?

The answer used to be, "Let's do an employee survey to find out." That happened perhaps once a year, or every two years, and it created an awful lot of work, generating a lot of data that was too general, outdated or, to be frank, inaccurate. Michael Silverman at MD Silverman Research expressed it like this in his *The Future of Employees* research report:

"The days of the traditional employee survey are numbered. Giving someone a questionnaire with 50 to 100 tick boxes (occasionally with a comment box) is not only tedious, it's downright useless in identifying any sort of meaningful action or response. Organizations have become so obsessed with scores on employee surveys that they have completely lost sight of what they surely set out to do: listen to their people."

The exact reason Inpulse was created was as a better way to listen to people and to involve them, with a greater share of their hearts and minds, in the enterprise. This book was written to share the direction and approach we think engagement is going and present case studies that show what we're learning from this new approach. To be absolutely clear, we want to challenge that old way of thinking and encourage others to shift towards a better approach. What has been set out here will not be the last word on the subject, and an iterative process of collaboration is very much welcomed; this will ultimately lead to better knowledge, fuller engagement and, yes, change. So I hope readers will share their experiences and insights with me in this spirit. We can all learn from each other.

As long as I've been involved in employee engagement, measuring it has always been more of an art than a science. Today the continuum has, at one end, the very simplistic daily 'mood monitor' that asks people whether they feel happy, sad or mad; at the other end of the continuum is the long, traditional survey, asking too many questions and too few questions that truly engage with people's real feelings.

There Is a Better Way

On the one hand, the 'always-on' surveys lead to data overload and, therefore, lost opportunities. They make it difficult to be clear about what it all means and difficult to hear what people are really saying. That, in turn, makes it difficult to take action and, because the process is not engaging, counterproductive. It can lead to low response rates because people feel overwhelmed by the daily request to fill out a survey. Rather than being engaged, there is a risk that people feel interrogated.

On the other hand, the annual/bi-annual surveys create the problem of minimal listening, with maximal data. They produce analytics that are rinsed dry over a period well beyond their expiration date. It is at best pointless to use out-of-date analytics and at worst dangerous, as it gives the impression of not listening properly, leading to people feeling alienated. The data reflects a time that is past; it is no longer what people are thinking and feeling now or even recently.

The Inpulse approach is different. It is somewhere in be-tween the always-on and the once-a-year survey, a tool to use to identify the rhythm and pulse when required. Through the case studies, I've tried to show that Inpulse is the 21st century way, one that gives you good analytics and good usage because you're listening and involved regularly, but not excessively. It is linked to the employee experience and encourages the kind of engagement that ultimately creates strong business impact.

The case studies show how Inpulse can provide data and insight beyond employee engagement, to areas like employee experience, cultural dynamics, understanding and alignment to the organization's goals and strategy, perception of communications and of leadership, and reaction to business changes that might be happening.

In companies using Inpulse, the results now affect the direction of the business and the ongoing decisions of leaders. The real-time data is beginning to be used to help drive the business forward. It's a long way from the traditional approach of fitting the analytics into some simplistic categories like 'say, stay and strive'.

Inpulse has proved to me, and clearly to the blue-chip clients using it, that companies are looking for new ways of understanding and measuring the key issues around employee engagement and experience. The trend emerging is towards better measurement of emotional sentiment within organizations. This data must be simple and usable, so that managers and their teams can immediately use it to have conversations about what it means – and then, most importantly, what needs to happen because of it.

Inpulse started life being about emotion and the question 'why'. It is now being used in two main ways by companies. The first way is as the means to measure engagement on a regular basis, using an agreed-upon index. Vitally, these questions include how people feel. This provides the benchmark for the company to see whether they are improving or not, how and why.

The second way took me a little by surprise. It has become the tool for companies to track how people feel about their town halls, their change programmes, their employee experience, their learning and development programmes, their leadership events and their cultural elements. In other words, they use it as a way to listen to their people; and this enables them to make decisions, take action and drive the business forward. I was surprised at the speed of that outcome, only two years into the development of Inpulse.

And, as the icing on the cake, it's extremely pleasing that all Inpulse clients believe that it has made the means of gathering employee insight more engaging – design does matter!

This new approach to engagement is the future. But why is that so?

I suggest seven principles, which apply to companies, that will challenge existing mindsets about engagement.

1. 'Why should I care how people feel?'

The question is real. It came from a senior leader recently when we were talking about how to develop high performance teams. His concern was that we were asking them to focus on making people happy, when what the business strongly needed was to increase productivity. He thought we were being fluffy, when he needed us to be focused. It was a fair challenge. We responded by explaining that how we feel has a massive impact on what we do which, in turn, affects the outcomes we get. We are all driven far more by emotion than most of us like to admit – Daniel Kahneman's work into how we make decisions has shown this. Far from being ancillary, truly understanding how people are feeling and why can give any organization a huge lever in improving output and performance.

This is what led us into the whole area of emotional analytics in the first place – because no one was really helping organizations get to grips with emotions – and to develop Inpulse to do just that. Every Inpulse survey starts with the question "How do you feel about...?" Participants are then invited to select two emotions from a range of nine offered, the list being tailored to fit the issue or topic in question.

This information provides valuable insight into people's emotional state. Inpulse has been widely used over the last three years across a variety of sectors: retail, publishing, academia, technology, household goods, manufacturing and finance. It's been applied to run pulse checks, full blown opinion surveys, reactions to changes, making town halls interactive and to review coaching workshops. In fact, for many clients, Inpulse has become more than the survey tool. It has come to describe a whole approach where organizations start with people's emotions when trying to understand issues in meetings and day-to-day conversations, as well as in surveys.

From all the surveys we have helped clients run and analyse, we now have a very useful and comprehensive array of data. These surveys are from different organizations, designed and carried out for different reasons, each with different populations. Nonetheless, it has been fascinating to add up all the emotions selected in each of these surveys to see what they tell us. It gives us a fascinating snapshot and insight into how people are feeling about their work and organizations. It also provides useful figures to use for benchmarking.

Let's start with the overall picture. In terms of emotions selected, it's pretty much level pegging – out of 41 emotions, 21 are positive and 20 are negative. However, the positive emotions tend to have been selected more frequently than the negatives – some of which were only chosen a handful of times. Overall then, it seems like good news – people at work are generally more engaged and positive than not.

So far, so good. But, if they are engaged, why is that? The top three selected positive emotions may help explain this. They are enthusiastic, motivated and inspired. The responses to the 'why' question suggest that, in a lot of cases, leaders are getting their messages about their vision and strategies through – it's hard to be any of these things if you don't know where you are heading and how you will get there. It's also worth noting that those organizations where the most frequently selected emotions were enthusiastic and motivated were also fast growing. The next three positive are empowered, confident and valued, which also indicates that leaders have been successful in helping many people take responsibility, try out new things and be recognized for successes.

It's not all good news, though, as alongside these positives are two high scoring negatives – disconnected and disappointed. This indicates that there is little room for complacency and that leaders still need to do more to help everyone feel part of what's happening in their organization, and get behind it. Even when strategy and vision are clear, the 'why' question again shows that the majority of people still feel unmoved by it and are yet to see what part they can play and how it will help them. This is reinforced as we look a little lower down the list at the next negatives. Apprehensive and anxious indicate that a sizeable number of people find themselves in uncertain and unfamiliar circumstances in which they are unlikely to perform at their best, while demotivated, uninterested, negative and plain bored are all high scores for such destructive emotions. This highlights lost opportunities to capture people's imagination and the discretionary effort that goes with it.

Before we become too gloomy, there is good news at the other end of the scale. There are low scores for intimidated, manipulated and upset. This is important because these negative emotions tend to be those caused by bullying and deliberate bad behaviour by leaders. The low scores suggest that managing by fear and command and control is in decline.

Given the importance of emotions in determining performance, those we have seen expressed by people in Inpulse surveys so far suggest movement in the right direction. They are more positive than negative, and indicate high levels of understanding, belonging and empowerment. Organizations also seem to be appreciating the value of good leadership, as the impact of bad behaviour by bosses is relatively low. Leaders still have their work cut out, though, and they must continue to work on making connections, explaining implications and helping people see how they can contribute.

2. 'Why' Focuses the Mind

How do people feel in the moment? We need to know. Even more crucially, we need to know 'why'. Understanding why gives you the content for the conversation, and the conversation allows you to listen, and the listening gives you understanding, and from that point you can move people's emotions by responding.

Inpulse has proved, through hundreds of surveys, that the 'why' gives you what employees are focused on and, therefore, what is enabling or blocking a good experience. With the 'why', you can easily focus on what is really important to the employee, not what you think is important. We need to move away from conjecture and the old management lines of, "I think they feel that way because ..." or "The annual survey three months ago said they felt that way because ...."

It's also a matter of speed and efficiency. Through the question 'why', we can not only understand issues better but also pinpoint the vital issues more quickly.

Inpulse has taught us that when minimizing the number of words used in a question, similar to Twitter, people answer the 'why' questions much more pithily, revealing more. The more you listen, the more people open up. Freed from the pressure of writing something completely thought through, knowing that there's no need to write *War and Peace*, people write sentences packed with emotion and meaning.

3. Heed the Lessons of Technology

Twitter is one example of how technology has changed our ways of thinking and communicating. Although we live with 21st century technology, most companies still often use 20th century thinking. There is much we can learn from social media, in particular. We are, with some sense of shock, realizing that even the President of the United States communicates through social media. People working in companies now have social media as a natural part of their everyday lives, and that has happened because they enjoy it. We should learn from that.

People use social media because they relish its ability to be instant, emotive, informative and expressive. They also find it easy to use and have taken to it very quickly, particularly with its need for brevity. As a result, we have all become accustomed to understanding more concise communications.

When asked "How do you feel?", people are honest and quickly revealing. This saves a huge amount of time and effort for managers trying to work it out by reading reams of free text answers that could amount to a book. It saves time and leads to better conversations.

Behind social media are technological principles, too, that we can learn and adapt from. Natural language processing allows us to drive harder into the words that people use in surveys. We realized that too much time might be wasted analysing answers to free text questions, so now we have developed algorithms that identify the most representative comments. This gives a snapshot for understanding the issues almost instantly. This came about because a leading grocer challenged us – "Our hundreds of branch managers don't have time to read all this." – so we responded with a simpler response that gets to the heart of the issue quicker.

This means we can analyse language sentiment, not just language – the themes as well as the individual words. This even allows us to highlight positive and negative feelings clearly. At the moment we are testing this and it is working; this is a field of fast-moving innovation. The outcome should be that we will be able to spend more time talking about the root causes, rather than trying to work them out over much longer periods. As well as the analysis and the words, we will also be changing the visualization, so that everyone can understand unmistakably what others are feeling, giving us a much richer input to conversations and decisions.

Being able to segment your results in whichever way you want is also critical. To name but a few, is there a difference between gender, age, hierarchical level or geography? Inpulse gives the ability to take an online view of different segments of the audience. This allows you to track different themes or issues pertinent to a certain group, which means your response can be more tailored and personal. It also means the CEO can immediately look at the segmentation report, see where has the most negative emotions, the reasons why and can then speak to the leader of that area about the issues. This is an approach we are finding more leaders are adopting as they realize the real-time nature of Inpulse and the ease with which they can see results by segments for the whole organization report.

4. Transparency Counts

Inpulse brings a fundamental commitment to transparency. Results appear instantly; they are up on a screen and they cannot be hidden. That is hard for some companies, particularly for some managers and leaders. We have had to give support to help leaders live with transparency.

The reason is obvious. There is fear that they will be blindsided or caught out by not having a good response. For some it's because they got to this point in their working life by managing in a more formal, hierarchical style. For others they are used to receiving the information days earlier than anyone else and being prepped so that they appear in the best possible light. We can all understand the hesitancy.

However, there are now many leaders who have come to love the transparency and the conversations it stimulates. When leaders engage in this way, people and teams also enjoy higher levels of involvement and trust. Every aspect of life is now becoming more transparent, and this is not a movement that is going to disappear: embrace it, don't fear it. Transparency leads to better, clearer, faster and simpler conversations and, when this possibility is embraced, it works for everyone in the business, including the leaders.

5. You Need to Build Trust

There is a clear link between commitment to transparency and trust: the sooner you embrace transparency, the faster you build trust. Every brand consultant will tell you that brands have to earn trust; they cannot claim it as a value or a right. It is a prize for every brand, for every business, and for every leader to aspire to. But how do you gain it? First, as a leader, you have to give it.

Management and leadership have changed dramatically over the last decade. Now people in companies expect more autonomy, and they are not looking to their manager to command and control how and what they do. On the contrary, they expect to be empowered, supported through swift decision-making and given resources that they need to achieve an objective. They want to be aligned and focused on what they need to achieve, but autonomous to work out how best to do what they need to do.

Inpulse aligns with this new leadership approach. It's about empowering people to share how they feel in a safe and transparent way about real-time issues, to gather feedback on their experience as that is happening, and for leaders to listen as they lead.

In his book *The Happy Manifesto*, Henry Stewart talks about the importance of trust and freedom in creating happy employees. Picking up the story, he says:

"At one recent conference, I gave three options to a mixed group of hundreds of people. Which would they prefer?

Complete freedom: 7%
Freedom within clear guidelines: 89%
Be told what to do: 4%

People rarely ask to be given free rein. Instead, the most common comment is 'give us clear guidelines and then give us the freedom to work within them'."

This is a massive strategic shift in thinking and will require a huge mindset and skillset change from managers over the next decade. And it's one we're seeing highlighted time and again through Inpulse. The fact is, micromanagement causes strong negative emotional responses that result in disengagement and a loss of productivity.

Leaders should see this as an exciting opportunity, as long as they can abandon outdated views of leadership. It need no longer be 'lonely at the top'. Leaders can gain the full benefits of leading a team. That team is there to help them, and it can be an extended team of many talents, because we all recognize that no individual leader can have all the skills.

So leaders can be helped to develop the right mindset (I have nothing to fear from knowing how people feel), skillset (I know how to manage myself and others appropriate to their emotional state), and toolset (Inpulse results enable me to facilitate open, enjoyable conversations. I know how to listen and respond).

There is also the earlier point that every manager needs to be a leader of a team these days. The manager's job is no longer about ticking the box of a process. This is a new challenge and, if embraced, it energizes all the people of a business.

This is the 21st century role of every manager. We still have a long way to go, but we are clearly moving in that direction.

6. Give Your People a Voice

As discussed in Chapter 2, stronger 'employee voice' in an organization leads to greater levels of employee engagement. Transparency, openness and immediacy enable employees to be heard and ultimately lead to a more democratic workplace. I write these words now, certain that at the end of this decade, these will be the accepted operating methods of business.

Today there is still a whiff of revolution about stating such thoughts – hence the title of this book. But revolutions need not be violent; they can be benign. I believe in it, because the principles I am advocating through Inpulse represent a win-win situation in the modern business world. They are empowering for leaders, managers and every contributor to a business, whether on the 'shop floor' (as some businesses still term it), for the part-time workers, and for the suppliers and consultants and partners who work with the business. All have a vested interest in the business's future, and Inpulse is simply a tool that helps move towards that future.

Whether through a transformation programme at Time Inc. or the future values of ASOS, Inpulse has enabled employees to be consulted and to communicate their views. Of course, it went further than that, because employees were influencing the leadership. And the leaders were appreciating that this was a positive, creative force.

Giving a more regular voice leads to higher levels of trust in senior leaders, as everyone recognizes and gives credit to the bravery – but common sense – of making results transparent.

It also helps to strengthen team relationships, as managers have more real-time insight to discuss with their teams. This is crucial for engagement and business generally, as it develops a much deeper and two-way sense of trust. Without trust, you don't get very far or get much done; people won't follow you, flow with change or give their best. The result is less scepticism, more genuine empowerment. Conversations empower employees to work out what needs to be changed or communicated differently.

7. Is Your Approach Synthetic or Organic?

If there is one thing we've learned – and it should hardly seem such a secret – it's that there is a 21st century business imperative to be more organic, to communicate more naturally and timely, to have a conversation in the moment and not when it's scheduled in three months' time. You might think this is a message that has been around for all time, and you are right. But for all the reasons set out above, not least technological changes and accompanying attitudinal changes, we now operate in a completely new environment, where people want an approach to surveys and insight that feels organic; human rather than machine-like and synthetic.

The first principle every leader and manager has bowed down to for the last hundred years in business life is the importance of face-to-face communication. Face-to-face communication is far more effective at sorting out those issues of credibility and trust, and should allow for an organic solution. But it is not always available – there is simply not enough time. As a result, too many people complain that they haven't been communicated with about a new strategy, the company's development, etc. Or they complain it feels false, too unnatural and lacking emotional truth. In other words, people don't always feel it and the answer to leaders is be more natural, timely and real.

Inpulse certainly doesn't make the whole organization organic, but it is a useful adjunct to it, not least because it is effectively an approach that creates more of a feeling of being human than the traditional approaches to engagement and surveys ever will. It links people directly, as individual to individual. Inpulse gives people the opportunity to air a grievance, perhaps in a way that is even easier and more effective than face-to-face. It enables everyone to be better at both listening and talking.

Because things have changed. Many corporate organizations still base the way they behave on the belief that everything works as a machine – a precise, well-ordered, predictable machine, with hierarchical structures, narrow incentivization and an obsession with measurement. But experience shows us that this approach is playing to the lowest common denominator and is self-destructive. It results in misunderstood incentives, failing change programmes and poor employee engagement.

Inpulse challenges organizations to re-examine how they see themselves: to see that they are much more interdependent, networked, human and relational. People want the places where they work to be more human and less like machines; more insight and less analysis; more emotion and less cold statistics; less standard more adaptable; less process-driven and more innovative; and less synthetic but more organic.

Inpulse is changing the way companies go about their engagement – from focusing on resources, objectives, scales and reviews to emotions, listening, conversations and outcomes. The focus is changing from hierarchy to participation, from how we solve things to why we need to solve them, from what people are thinking to how people are feeling.

This means that the whole style of communication needs to be reassessed and improved. If, as that modern mantra goes, 'we are all in this together', you need to show it.

The Very Last Word

An interesting lesson from Inpulse has been the need for more conversations and less action. While employees taking part in Inpulse expect action, what the insight showed is that they need conversation first. Most of the issues that Inpulse has highlighted across thousands of surveys comes down to the simple need to talk.

It does all start by talking, and it continues in that way. The 21st century way of working is collaboration, participation and partnership. If you've enjoyed reading this book, I'd love to hear from you. Let's talk. It could lead in an interesting direction.

CHAPTER

10

The World Is Changing Faster than I Thought!

It's been two years since I wrote the first edition of this book. What has changed in that time? It seemed like the right moment to address that and other questions because so much has changed.

Much like a pulse, the market in which we operate moves on steadily and, in recent times, increasingly rapidly. Inpulse clients operate in that market and it's from them, in particular, that I've been learning.

For me learning should always be constant. I've always found it to be the key to innovation, to business development, to always staying one step ahead. And I see Inpulse as a learning tool.

We called this edition of the book *The Engagement Revolution*. My publishers suggested that because they have seen, as players and influencers in the world of business, that the word 'revolution' is justified. With the first edition we used it perhaps a little tentatively – it seemed as if we might be overclaiming. But the experience of the last two years has given us the absolute right to say that this is an engagement revolution.

Many more clients have signed up with Inpulse and they are important companies. They want to engage more effectively with their employees because they are putting increasing value on that objective. They realized that the traditional means of doing so – annual surveys – were no longer cutting it. Inpulse was not an alternative to the annual survey. Instead, it represented a completely new way of going about their business. It was different, and significantly better, because it was a better way to manage and to *lead*.

Clients keep saying to me, "Inpulse captures what we were seeking and sensing – but were not certain of."

Those words seem simple but they say a lot because they show how the industry has changed. Within that statement, I'd suggest that there are two signs of change. First, we see a greater willingness among leaders to acknowledge doubt. It's become a truism: 'We live in uncertain times'. This is undoubtedly true – there's uncertainty all around – but leaders no longer feel such an overwhelming need to lead by demonstrating their own certainties, their own omnipotence. They have realized that they can be vulnerable and be seen to be vulnerable. That *human* quality in fact builds a connection with the people they lead. It does not undermine them through any perceived 'weakness' but adds to their standing because they are seen as strengthened by honesty. Honesty, authenticity, transparency – these are vital qualities for a leader to embrace and embody today.

The other word I draw attention to is 'sensing'. When I first approached potential clients about the value of pulsing surveys five years ago, it was a relatively hard sell to persuade business people that 'emotion' and 'emotional words' were relevant to the situations we were discussing. "How do you feel?" is the starting point for every survey we conduct. Emotion, feeling, sensing – words that were viewed with suspicion not long ago – have now entered the engagement mainstream.

The Inpulse approach incorporates emotional terms as central to the way it listens. People are asked directly if they feel committed or anxious, enthusiastic or disappointed, motivated or disengaged, inspired or bored, positive or negative. This encourages them to say how they truly feel. And that's significant, because that kind of honesty leads to better and more meaningful conversations. It's what makes us human, after all!

Those are two straws in the wind, and they indicate to me that the industry has changed so much in the last few years. The revolution has actually happened, and it's been a peaceful, positive revolution that has led companies to a better way of doing business with their own employees. Rather than the stock phrase that always sounded hollow – 'Our people are our greatest assets' – Inpulse demonstrates through every survey that your people have a voice and the leaders are listening, not just to their words but to their feelings as well.

As a result, the traditional annual survey now seems almost like a museum relic. Some companies still conduct them and they provide a lot of data – data that needs to be analysed at length. Time passes, so that when the analysis eventually appears the company's situation is inevitably different from when it was surveyed. Inpulse is loved because it is so quick. Those taking part can see it happening before their eyes. The questions are fewer and shorter and require less analysis, yet they point more clearly towards the need for action. So, rather than paralysis resulting from analysis, Inpulse enables clarity of understanding that leads to solidly grounded action.

The old style of survey was safe. It resided under the control of leadership teams and controversial views could be excluded, strong opinions sidelined. Inpulse is a revolution because its approach is bold and open; it takes a risk through its transparency. A manager cannot hide, but he or she can seize the opportunity to gain credibility by giving an honest response based on authentic, real-time data.

We were fortunate to find brave clients as early adopters. But those trailblazers have now become the mainstream. Everyone is now looking to pulse – pulse surveys have become accepted as the way to develop better employee engagement.

In fact, over the last five years very little has changed in the way we conduct Inpulse surveys. Our understanding has grown and led to significant product development: the software has become even better; the impulse to action has become stronger; and our ability to help management follow through on action plans has become much more focused and supportive. But at the heart of the system, the two questions that set the pulse going remain the same: "How do you feel about…?" and "Why?"

These days, when I start explaining Inpulse I find that clients are already talking to me about wanting to understand how their people are really feeling. There is no longer a slightly nervous hedging about it.

"We want to know because we know it is important."

As a result, the Inpulse business now has many more clients and we have grown in terms of our employees, services and scope of activities. We've become comfortable being a tech company and an engagement consultancy – it's who and what we are. Like any consultancy, we learn from every new client and the value added is passed on to innovative new developments we can offer future clients. Fostering learning development within our clients' organizations is a crucial objective for us. We have developed e-books, video tutorials and coaching for team members as part of the ongoing drive towards effective action.

All this ties in with the values we see as intrinsic to Inpulse:
- Take ownership
- Build relationships
- Be our best selves
- Surprise, delight and enjoy the journey

I've spelled these out here because, although they are Inpulse's internal values, they show the truths that underlie our approach, and it is helpful for others to understand them. The first is all about taking the initiative to achieve positive results, caring and being accountable. The second is about being transparent and gaining trust through inclusion, connection and community. The third, which is particularly personal to me, is about pursuing our dreams, trying new things and not becoming complacent. Finally, the fourth is about getting to know our clients as individuals – understanding their wishes, hopes and needs – while finding the good in each day and having a laugh along the way.

These are core values for my business. They won't be replicated in every client we work with; each client has its own set of values. But my belief is that each business that adopts Inpulse will feel a sense of connection to these ideals. They are part of ongoing conversations we have with our clients, because Inpulse is much more than a data-gathering survey. It is a powerful means of nudging behavioural change from managers and leadership teams. The focus on change that is inherent to Inpulse makes it an ideal tool for these times, when change management is the dominant issue in much of corporate life.

The change in the overall landscape means that pulse surveys are now seen as normal and natural, because they have been proven to be such a useful tool. With new clients now, the questions are not about the fundamental philosophy but about practical issues. Over the last two years, for instance, one of the most common questions has been about frequency. We have tried many different options, and our view is that regularity matters. However, surveying too frequently might not allow sufficient time for follow-up reflection, analysis and effective action. So, we generally recommend a quarterly rather than a monthly survey.

This is because we are getting into some deep issues much of the time. We're probing matters rooted in culture and individual behaviour, as well as addressing significant questions that all businesses want to know: How do we drive higher performance in the organization? How do we attract the best candidates? What can we do to boost sales and productivity? The list goes on, and it's growing daily.

One aspect of all this that I find interesting is that we are using technology, including AI, with a specific and very human purpose. The technology is advanced, and Inpulse could not operate without it, but our objective is simply to support better human conversations. We want to get people talking – not small talk, but meaningful dialogue about what really matters to them. What matters to them will inevitably matter to the business because these are the people you rely on to keep the business moving forward.

This has led, in turn, to deeper conversations that we now have with the leaders of businesses. We aim to support leaders after surveys, helping them to think through what the surveys are telling them and to devise and execute the right actions in response. It's a direction I had always anticipated, and wrote about in the first edition, but it's been reinforced by all our experiences. The simple question 'Why' remains central to everything we do. It's the basis for better conversations between our clients and us, and between employees and managers. The need for emotional intelligence is becoming greater, year to year, and pulsing is another aspect of that.

The other thing that has been changing is the culture and the social environment in which we work. The #MeToo movement has sprung up, there are important issues of LGBT identity, gender equality and respect for different faiths, belief systems and ways of being. These have all come closer to the mainstream in a way that wasn't entirely expected five years ago. Diversity & Inclusion is part of what we routinely survey now, and the results matter. The obvious thing to say about Inpulse is that it does not discriminate; it gives a voice to everyone within a client's business. Expression is better than suppression, and Inpulse can enable rich and rewarding conversations. And that means that all parts of a community are truly *engaged*. That has been a revolution.

I am interested in driving real change. My motivation is not financial. What gives me pleasure, what motivates me day after day, is the thought that we are making a difference. Of course, there are the usual business imperatives behind what we do – if we don't make a profit, we don't exist. But there is a deeper satisfaction when I work with a business and can see that real change results. This change isn't driven by financial analysis and smart accountancy;

it happens as a result of people becoming truly engaged in what they do during their hours at work.

We collect data, we analyse data and we respect the confidentiality of data because our focus is on the individuality of everyone taking part in a pulse survey. We make it easier for the individual voices to be heard and to play a part in the future direction of the organization where they work and invest so much of their energy and emotion. We start with emotion, and we unlock it in a positive way.

What more can I say? It works, and we have shown that it works.

It's *The Engagement Revolution.*

An Introduction
to Matt Stephens

Matt Stephens is a leading authority on the increasingly important organizational topics of employee engagement and experience. As founder of Quest Agency, a fast-growing consultancy, he is helping some of the UK's largest businesses navigate change by better harnessing the skills and energy of their people.

In 2014, he launched a groundbreaking employee engagement platform called Inpulse, which enables organizations to measure employee emotion in real time and is challenging traditional approaches to engagement by championing the importance of leaders making emotional connections with employees.

After graduating with a degree in Politics and International Relations, Matt began his career working client-side in employee communications with Norwich Union before establishing himself as an independent consultant. Over the next decade he acted as a trusted advisor to a wide span of organizations ranging from corporates such as the insurer RSA, to the energy firm E.ON, before founding Quest Agency in January 2012, a consultancy supporting organizational leadership, culture and engagement. Quest's clients include Allied Irish Bank, Heineken, Nokia and Unilever.

Outside work Matt is a keen golfer, skier and supporter of the anti-child trafficking charity, Love146.org, which he chairs. He lives in Hertfordshire with his wife and three football-mad sons.